## A Message of Hope to the People of New Orleans

**From**

Beverly Choltco-Devlin

**Who lives in**

Hamilton, NY

**On this day**

We are thinking of you up in NewYork State

Rebuild

NEW ORLEANS
PUBLIC LIBRARY

LK

# Acts of Light

UNIVERSITY PRESS OF FLORIDA

*Florida A&M University, Tallahassee*

*Florida Atlantic University, Boca Raton*

*Florida Gulf Coast University, Ft. Myers*

*Florida International University, Miami*

*Florida State University, Tallahassee*

*University of Central Florida, Orlando*

*University of Florida, Gainesville*

*University of North Florida, Jacksonville*

*University of South Florida, Tampa*

*University of West Florida, Pensacola*

# Acts of Light

## Martha Graham in the Twenty-first Century

PHOTOGRAPHS BY JOHN DEANE

TEXT BY NAN DEANE CANO

UNIVERSITY PRESS OF FLORIDA

Gainesville · Tallahassee · Tampa · Boca Raton
Pensacola · Orlando · Miami · Jacksonville · Ft. Myers

Text copyright 2006 by Nan Deane Cano

Photographs copyright 2006 by John Deane

Printed in China on acid-free paper

11  10  09  08  07  06   6  5  4  3  2  1

A record of cataloging-in-publication data is available
from the Library of Congress.

ISBN 0-8130-2992-9

The University Press of Florida is the scholarly
publishing agency for the State University System of
Florida, comprising Florida A&M University, Florida
Atlantic University, Florida Gulf Coast Univer-
sity, Florida International University, Florida State
University, University of Central Florida, University
of Florida, University of North Florida, University of
South Florida, and University of West Florida.

University Press of Florida
15 Northwest 15th Street
Gainesville, FL 32611-2079

http://www.upf.com

*For our parents,*
*John Joseph Deane*
*and*
*Margaret Lynch Mahler Deane,*
*Le grá*
*With love*

# Contents

# Foreword

John Deane's photographs of the twenty-first century's Martha Graham Dance Company, presented on the following pages, represent a fresh, clear-eyed, highly sophisticated, faux-naïve, contemporary look at young dancers dancing some of the great twentieth-century works created by the legendary American choreographer Martha Graham. The photographs were taken during the past three years.

While John is relatively new to dance photography, his experience as a fine-art photographer prepared him with an aptitude adaptable for pursuing dance photography. He simply photographs dance as the fine art it is, adds the illusion of motion, and retains the integrity of the choreography and its creator. He is an artist.

I have seen and photographed most of the ballets shown here, some with the original cast. It is with this credential that I recommend these dance photographs to you. Look, linger, and enjoy the timeless brilliance of Graham dance as performed, exclusively for John Deane's camera, by the world-class dancers of the revived Martha Graham Dance Company.

Jack Mitchell

June 2, 2005

# Artistic Directors' Statements

*On May 9, 2002, the Martha Graham Dance Company triumphantly returned to the stage after a two-year interruption forced upon them by legal challenges to their rights to perform Martha Graham's body of work. Artistic directors Christine Dakin and Terese Capucilli reflect on the Company, the dancers, and Martha's work.*

Since we began this period of the Company's rebirth, we have been inspired by the passion and talent of our new generation of dancers.

Most not having worked with Martha or seen her, they are finding their way into the work for the first time, drawn by the power of the dances and the technique that is the core of those dances.

We have come through the lost years' pain and challenges, when we sought any opportunities to dance—finding means and places to perform and giving the new dancers ways to grow into the dances again.

The company as individuals grew—and grew together to be a company, with us.

As we passed on our knowledge to them in new works and revived works not seen in a long time, we drew on our time with Martha and on the generation of dancers who shared with us their knowledge.

So we trust we are true to the integrity and scope of Martha's work as we know it.

The legacy is passed to every dance generation in the same way: by watching and working and teaching.

Notated only in the physical presence of the dancers' bodies, they learn by absorbing the ballets into their muscles and hearts.

We love being able to share with the dancers, being the guides for their growth.

We permit them, demand of them, a perfection, and that they find their own individuality in the repertory.

This work is about a passionate commitment and a demanding realism, coupled with a willingness, an eagerness, to look and work deeply, to take risks, as Martha's work requires.

And there is the spirit, the humanity of the artist, of the individual, at the core of what we do.

Terese Capucilli and Christine Dakin, artistic directors, Martha Graham Dance Company, 2001–2005

## Statement by Janet Eilber

How can any still photograph hope to depict the action and passion of the art of movement?

Perhaps an answer can be found in an enigmatic quotation from the poet Edward Varese that was one of Martha Graham's favorites: "We have so little time to be born to the instant." That thought had layers of meaning for her that evolved and deepened throughout her lifelong pursuit of the revelatory.

Those of us privileged to work closely with her were made keenly aware that the essence of dance exists only in what Martha called "the instant"—that fleeting moment of recognition when the dancer and the audience become one. She was dedicated to readying herself for that instant. By example and by direction, she infused us with a fierce commitment to the emotional and physical preparation that is vital to the fulfillment of that transformative moment.

One of my most powerful memories of Martha was in a rehearsal for *Night Journey*, her masterpiece

Janet Eilber

As she walked back to her chair she repeated, "You simply must talk to yourself the whole time," and added, "I think I used to do it rather automatically."

I remember being stunned. In a few simple sentences, she had revealed the secret to her legendary performances—her key to being "in the moment."

Soon onstage, I remember being propelled almost without effort through that difficult solo, the movement driven not by the memorization of the physical steps but by the haunting emotional preparation of every move—of every instant.

This book of John Deane's photographs gives us insight to both the instant and the personal dedication that are so much a part of Martha's aesthetic. Because of his artistry and understanding of the work, his photos catch and preserve the energy and visible intensity of the dancers who have worked to ready themselves for their breakthrough moments.

The narrative by Nan Cano, and especially her interviews with the memorable Graham dancers, provide a glimpse of the intense personal preparation required of these artists (how they "talk to themselves" as they dance) and enhance the reader's understanding of what is shown in Deane's photographs.

We are fortunate that their collaboration has made it possible for so many superb dancers to have their work documented both in high points of movement and in their own words. Dancers of the future will grasp what has been captured here. They will recognize, as Martha Graham did, how excitingly essential it is to make the most of the time we have "to be born to the instant."

Janet Eilber
Artistic Director
The Martha Graham Center

based on the story of Oedipus. We were alone in the studio. She had asked me, on very short notice, to step into the role that years before had been hers: Jocasta, the woman fated to be both mother and wife to Oedipus. I was in my early thirties. Martha was ninety and unable to demonstrate the physical moves dancing in her mind. She used all her powers of description and inspiration to imbue me with her concept of this role, arguably her most challenging. She watched me perform the opening solo, full of wild runs that zigzag from one point to another in the setting Isamu Noguchi had devised as Jocasta's bedroom. Then she got up from her chair and slowly walked over to where I was recovering—out of breath and spent.

"You have to talk to yourself, darling," she said quietly. "You have to talk to yourself the whole time. You arrive at this spot and you say, 'this is where I weaned him as a babe . . . ,' and you can't possibly stay there. You find yourself at another spot and say, 'this is where he took me as a lover . . . ,' and you can't possibly stay there either. You are not *going* anywhere, darling—you are *leaving*."

# Acknowledgments

As my sister and I reflect on our years of collaboration blending words and photographs to reflect the genius of Martha Graham and her Company, we gratefully enumerate our acknowledgments to all those who helped and inspired us.

The first person within the Graham organization to whom I broached the idea of the book was the then artistic director of resources, Janet Eilber, whose gracious encouragement and advice set us on the right course. Even before that, though, I had already developed a close working relationship with the two artistic directors of the Martha Graham Dance Company, Terese Capucilli and Christine Dakin. It is difficult to describe adequately what it meant to collaborate with two such superlative artists whom I had so often admired onstage. Throughout most of the three years I spent photographing the dances portrayed in these pages, Christine and Terese performed before my camera and then sat down beside me, offering discerning words of guidance, appreciation, and enthusiasm. It was an empowering experience.

And so it was to work with all the dancers of the Company, who made Nan and me feel like part of their family. The rapport we developed brought me closer to grasping the essence of dance and through them even, perhaps, to knowing something of one of the greatest artists of the twentieth century, Martha Graham. They were all unstinting in their dedication and professionalism to the work at hand, and Nan and I deeply appreciate the way they opened their hearts and souls to Nan, as the reader will find is evidenced in the text.

In particular I owe a lifetime debt of gratitude to principal dancer Miki Orihara and her husband, Stephen Pier, steadfast friends who were the first to awaken in me the joy of photographing dance. Armed with a portfolio of my new dance photos, Miki lobbied relentlessly to introduce me to Marvin Preston, the executive director of the Martha Graham Center of Contemporary Dance, whose wizened hand was essential in setting me on this path with the Company. Words of encouragement from Francis Mason, the Center chairman, added confidence to our endeavors. Marni Thomas helped enormously with stories of the early days with Martha Graham and her work with the Graham School of Dance. Jeffrey Wirsing and Karen Young faithfully brought their prodigious skills and artistry with the Graham costumes to all of our photo sessions.

Special thanks are due to Nobue Hirabayashi, whose beautiful design of the book's presentation caught the eyes and won the praise of Meredith Morris-Babb and the other good folks at our publisher, the University Press of Florida. I would be remiss if I did not thank Thomas Cano, whose succinct legal advice has guided me through a series of negotiations that laid the foundation for bringing my work to a larger audience.

I am confident that all the Martha Graham dancers and everyone associated with the Company management will join me in expressing our sincere thanks to Benoit Lagarde, the co-owner of Splashlight Studios, for donating time at the most luxurious and professionally appointed photography studios in New York. A creative atmosphere is key to any photo session, and Benoit and his employees provided us this time and time again.

I am also truly and deeply appreciative of the unbridled praise and encouragement from the greatest dance photographer ever, bar none, my dear friend, Jack Mitchell. When someone of Jack's caliber waxes eloquent about you, you take notice.

Finally, I gladly praise the author, my sister, Nan. It has been a privilege and a joy to work with her from start to happy finish. Having this opportunity brought to fruition is a source of pride for us both, be it somewhat tinged with melancholy for not having our parents here to share it with us.

John Deane

# Chronology of Dances Studied in *Acts of Light*

*Lamentation*
Music by Zoltán Kodály
*Premiere: January 8, 1930*

*Primitive Mysteries*
Music by Louis Horst
Premiere: February 2, 1931

*Deep Song*
Music by Henry Cowell
Premiere: December 19, 1937

*El Penitente*
Music by Louis Horst
Premiere: August 11, 1940

*Deaths and Entrances*
Music by Hunter Johnson
Premiere: July 18, 1943

*Appalachian Spring*
Music by Aaron Copland
Premiere: October 30, 1944

*Herodiade*
Music by Paul Hindemith
Premiere: October 30, 1944

*Dark Meadow*
Music by Carlos Chavez
Premiere: January 23, 1946

*Cave of the Heart*
Music by Samuel Barber
Premiere: May 10, 1946

*Errand into the Maze*
Music by Gian Carlo Menotti
Premiere: February 28, 1947

*Night Journey*
Music by William Schuman
Premiere: May 3, 1947

*Diversion of Angels*
Music by Norman Dello Joio
Premiere: August 13, 1948

*Embattled Garden*
Music by Carlos Surinach
Premiere: April 3, 1958

*Phaedra*
Music by Robert Starer
Premiere: March 4, 1962

*Circe*
Music by Alan Hovhaness
Premiere: September 6, 1963

*Acts of Light*
Music by Carl Nielsen
Premiere: February 26, 1981

"Spectre-1914" from *Sketches from Chronicle*
Music by Wallingford Riegger
Reconstruction 1989

*Satyric Festival Song*
Original Music by Imre Weisshaus
Music for Reconstruction by Fernando Palacios
Arranged by Aaron Sherber 1994

# The Dancers

The Martha Graham Dance Company in 2002–2005

| Dancer | Year Joined | Dancer | Year Joined |
|---|---|---|---|
| Christine Dakin | 1976 | Brenda Nieto | 2002 |
| Terese Capucilli | 1979 | Heidi Stoeckley | 2002 |
| Kenneth Topping | 1985 | Yuko Suzuki | 2002 |
| Miki Orihara | 1987 | Blakeley White-McGuire | 2002 |
| Elizabeth Auclair | 1993 | David Zurak | 2002 |
| Katherine Crockett | 1993 | Whitney Hunter | 2003 |
| Gary Galbraith | 1993 | Maurizio Nardi | 2003 |
| Martin Lofsnes | 1993 | Gelan Lambert Jr. | 2004 |
| Alessandra Prosperi | 1993 | | |
| Virginie Victoire Mécène | 1994 | | |
| Fang-Yi Sheu | 1995 | | |
| Tadej Brdnik | 1996 | | |
| Erica Dankmeyer | 1996 | | |
| Christophe Jeannot | 1998 | | |
| Jennifer Depalo-Rivera | 1999 | | |
| Jennifer Conley | 2002 | | |
| Carrie Ellmore-Tallitsch | 2002 | | |
| Kim Jones | 2002 | | |
| Catherine Lutton | 2002 | | |
| Ritsa Mavrokefalou | 2002 | | |

# Introduction

*"Desire is a lovely thing, and that is where
the dance comes from, from desire."*
*—Martha Graham*

What did the lithe young girl desire? To move and breathe freely—not the norm for a girl born in 1894. Martha Graham experienced family losses as a child and knew emptiness. All her joys and sorrows melted into her body and remained where she could touch them for ninety-seven years.

At fourteen, when Martha and her family moved from Pittsburgh to Santa Barbara, California, she ran the length of the train as the deep colors and immeasurable frontier landscape swept over her. The parallel tracks marched to infinity. The ballet *Frontier* began on that train in the mind of this American genius who wanted to capture America's space and rhythm.

How to make motion visible? How to blend memory, movement, and intuition in a dancer's body?

*"It all begins with the breath."*—Martha Graham

Transforming the simple in and out of breath, both gentle and fierce, Graham pulls movement from the body as if for the first time.

*Contraction. Release.*

*Contraction. Release.*

From such pure and natural resources, Martha crafted her technique like a Pueblo potter sinking her hands deep into rich clay awaiting her hands' powerful embrace. From the 1930s to the 1980s, the dances poured forth. We see her white face, a mask, glowing from the folds of a black gown stretched over and around her, creating a second skin, a private place. She asks if we are ready to go on life's journey with her, aware that pain undoubtedly awaits.

Just as Shakespeare compliments his audience by writing the words and simply giving them to us, Graham takes her audience by the hand, leading them to move, dance, feel, trusting their minds and souls would open, would know.

Graham's invitation echoes the most serious themes of the twentieth century. Her social consciousness gave voice to her new vocabulary: mothers losing sons in war after war, the depression, insidious mechanization informed her work. She heard voices; women spoke to her through time: Clytemnestra, Jocasta, Phaedra, Joan of Arc, Emily Dickinson. She danced into the paintings of Chagall, Picasso, Kandinsky, the sculptures of Calder and Noguchi. Danced into the farmhouses of a newly wed Shaker couple. Skipped through giddy and mature love, collapsed in pain.

Martha Graham knew she was a vessel for light and dark, destined to breathe in and out, to fall only to rise.

From 1926 on, dancers planted bare feet flat on the floor, gripped with arms, legs, bent torsos, and went deep into primal contractions and release. If audiences let themselves wander into her mazes, houses, streets, they find themselves waiting.

Life cuts, burns, freezes and laughs out loud. So does the Graham body of work of 181 ballets.

She was a golden treasure, hidden deep in many boxes. America and the world opened each box thinking the dances would never end. They did not. A new generation of dancers comes to the body of work with intensity gleaned from their own lives and their deep understanding of the blood memory that binds us all.

Today's company takes center stage as students of life, dancing in acts of light.

*And . . . one . . .*

# 1. *Appalachian Spring*

Today.

I have a husband.

I am a wife.

This is our first day in our new home.

I want it to be a perfect place for this mysterious man I love and for me.

I know he loves this spot, this soil, and I trust him, whatever lies ahead.

But today? Today I jump for joy!

So thinks the bride in our American treasure, *Appalachian Spring,* Martha's most generous gift to each of us. The work beckons the viewer to stand on this spot on this day and, in a singular moment, absorb all that is sweet and good about America.

It's coffee and small birds at dawn.

Light as a summer breeze moving through heat.

It is unhurried.

There is time for awakening.

Open spaces stretch forever.

Possibilities.

Commitment. Endurance.

And thigh-slapping laughter.

In her Americana series of works composed in the 1940s, Martha Graham joins the reflective artists of her time like Aaron Copland and Agnes de Mille, who had only to look around them to see a spirit that war could not eradicate.

In a remarkably trusting collaboration, Aaron Copland and Martha communicated by letters from 1942 to 1944 on a work originally meant to encompass the full span of American history. That daunting task narrowed itself to Copland's haunting, gently evocative *Ballet for Martha—Appalachian Spring.* Not intentionally about Appalachia at all, the name derives from a Harte Crane poem that Martha borrowed. It fit. In a letter to arts patron Elizabeth Sprague Coolidge in 1944, Martha wrote, "Some things happen to our mothers and some things happen to us, but they all happen to us. These happenings flow from generation to generation in succession and we are familiar with them. Such memories flow through our hearts. This dance has to do with living in a new town, someplace where the first fence has gone up."

We hear soft, small sounds crying in a clarinet from far away, bird songs mimicked by a flute, sonorous cello, and lightly plucked strings.

A bride and groom come to their new home, and we listen to all gathered this spring morning.

## Miki Orihara as the Bride

When Miki Orihara looks into the eyes of her new husband, she smiles with delight and her small-boned body quivers with joy. "My turns and quick runs reflect on my love and eagerness for this man. I feel pretty, and my raised arms flutter up and down to say, 'This is my day!' There is a moment in the dance, however, where I do pause. We have danced in do-si-do style, and that signature movement repeats later in the piece. Moving from that, I have a solo, 'The Bride's Prayer,' where everyone is turned away, kneeling upstage; maybe they are not there, at least in my mind. I am someplace else, despite the noise and excitement. I go into myself and dream about the children to come. I hope I am up to all the challenges. My back arches, and when I release a contraction into full movement and come back to

this minute, some shifts parallel to the floor ground me again. Time and place changed with my head back. I have some doubts, my hands join in prayer many times, and so a touch from the Pioneer Woman reassures me. Darting back and forth across stage I bow and acknowledge everyone, hoping for more blessings. I fly to the Husbandman's arms again and again in the dance. Just his touch comforts me. It is hard to separate Martha's movements from what I feel. It is essential and all found in the breath, in my contractions and releases. When the Husbandman touches me on the shoulder in the closing moments, my erect back and raised head looking directly into the future all help me express peace, love, and trust. We will be fine."

### Tadej Brdnik as the Husbandman

"I love to dance this. I will do anything for this woman. Anything. I walk the land with firm steps, and I like the house, the view, the future. In this house we will raise our family, and all we need is each other. I dig my foot into the ground near the beginning. I feel the soil and know it. My dances are energetic, but I slow easily for moments with my bride. A firm handshake from the preacher sends me on my way."

Another Husbandman, David Zurak, looks back to his Croatian family roots on a farm, and that memory stirs him to be a "simple, primal man doing simple things with basic determination." Indeed, this masterwork stirs memories in each of us, some we never knew we had.

### Maurizio Nardi as the Revivalist

"When I arrive on this day, I want this beautiful bride to feel in control and live every minute. I have done this many times before, and when I leave this new farm, I will bless more new homes on the frontier, but each is special. This is not just a job for me. When I leap, I leap for God. I want everyone to be taken to heaven on my leap! There is a moment where I feel all of Martha's theories coming together: I move from the floor movements into an arching leap, using both earth and air. My eyes strain as I look for God.

"My arms point—and I remind everyone there as witnesses that you had better watch me, pay attention." The horizon Maurizio sees is that of eternity. Today's wedding is a harbinger of tomorrow's equally certain funeral.

### Christophe Jeannot as the Revivalist

The evangelical preacher quivers with his message of God and Satan. Perhaps working out demons of his own, especially as danced by Christophe Jeannot, he can hardly contain himself. "Martha's dramatic tension sits in the back, rests on our spine. My deep beliefs pull my torso out from my spine, and a quick series of shuddering contractions seems to ripple out of my arms and chest." He is fire, brimstone, viscerally full of the Lord, and his spiritual fervor ignites the eager passions of young girls who flock to him. Enraptured by his vigor and sexual undercurrents, the girls whirl passion, religion, and sex with blurred lines. For his part, however, Christophe's preacher is not lured by winsome girls. His focus is clear, although he is aware of their enraptured gazes. "I feel I narrate the story and I want to be present at all times, everywhere I look. So my active stillness must convey my full attention today." He wants the girls to look at his role as one who blesses and may someday bless them.

Christophe likes the couple beginning their life together today and says simply, "I trust them."

### The Bride as Danced by Virginie Victoire Mécène

I love this dance.

I come from a village in France and these people lived in my childhood. The village is not my village, but it is the village of my husband. The Pioneer Woman could be my aunt. She knows everybody, and she is going to reassure me. I meet the preacher and the women who will help me.

I can imagine the grass on the ground, the dirt pathway. There is the fence, but beyond the fence, where the audience is sitting, is a big valley. I can see far away. It is a big, big place. The space is liberating and free. So I look beyond the audience. I see everything. I smell the flowers. For me it is 1895. It is springtime, of course. I can feel the air—it's not too hot, it's not too cold. I can feel the little wings of birds flying.

When first I danced this piece, Christine told me, "This is not France!" I knew what she meant and had to discipline my movements to match the Puritan mood. I focused my movement around the chair, the simple Shaker chair: two lines and just a little simple suggestion for this chair.

The house—just a few walls and there you have the house. Much more is unnecessary. Use the minimum. So with all you bring to a role, you must channel it in the right direction. I touch the chair. I feel the wood. This journey is real for me. Every time I return, it is a homecoming. I love this place. My dress is beautiful and full, and when I touch the fabric I am joyous.

When I dance, I wonder who in my family, in my entourage, can be with me? I feel very comfortable. It is not strange. I have been here many times.

You see, I got married in Kansas. I came from France to dance in America and be part of Martha Graham's Company, and my own family was not there. My husband's father was a minister and so he married us. The women of the church all helped me. They gave me a shower. I didn't know any of them, and they gave me all those presents! All those people were there for me. She is so frightened. It is another country, this new country, new family. She loves the Husbandman, but it is strange and frightening at the same time. I can relate to all this. It is the same thing.

Beneath the joy of the dance, discipline is everything. Sometimes it is just in warming up, from waking up in the center of myself, from beyond, a place that I feel is from my past, from before, my ancestors. That is the beauty of it. Once you discover this deep center, you have it forever. It is you, and you really awaken something. Martha knew this, and I believe it.

Virginie Victoire Mécène as the Bride in *Appalachian Spring*

## The Pioneer Woman

Some Graham roles call for specific body types. With her elegant height and erect carriage, Katherine Crockett lends a perfect physical reality to the important Pioneer Woman. Mature and seasoned, this woman knows everything that is going to happen. "I send out great love to this couple," Katherine states. "I try to impart confidence and calm to them. I sense their anxiety, but I hope they can put it aside for today. When the Bride turns to me at several points, she always receives my blessing."

Heidi Stoeckley draws on personal experience when she has occasion to perform the role. Heidi recalls growing up in a small town in Oklahoma. Dance lessons were far away, and a patient father drove her for hours each way, several days a week, for ten years. Her lessons with Mrs. Phi Delta Lee Evans Neal nurtured her desire to dance forever. Phi Delta knew this and encouraged the young girl to leave home at fifteen to study in Virginia and later to apply to Juilliard. How eagerly Heidi called her mentor with the good news that she had been accepted at the school for the arts. The teacher said, "I know. You've been accepted at Juilliard. I read my Bible this morning, and my bookmark fell out. I knew then."

Heidi's first role with the Martha Graham Company was the Pioneer Woman. "She embodies my Oklahoma teacher, and I see her every time I dance.

She was part Native American. She knew I had been assigned the role, and in her last letter to me she wrote her farewell as 'this Pioneering Woman.' I danced the role for the first time the month she died at 99." Heidi has fully integrated her teacher's devotion and certainty into her interpretation of the role. Long, majestic strides mark the woman's movements across stage, all with head erect, shoulders squared, back perfectly straight. "I pull the tailbone down to achieve that weighted walk. Elongate the spine and make space between the vertebrae with the release. I heard once that Martha had said that walking and standing are the most difficult things on stage. I agree!"

In the dance, she sits and watches. She touches the couple in a blessing. Her achingly sweet and holy solo says that she knows all that is ahead, and while it may be challenging, it is the texture of life really lived.

*The piece ends quite simply. It has the feeling of the town settling down for the night, the kind of thing that happens when one hears a call through the twilight,*
   *the voices of children in the distance,*
   *a dog barking,*
   *and then,*
     *night."*
—*Martha Graham*

The sun sets.

Girls whisper in the twilight.

Lights come on in a farm nearby and in this newest home.

Simple gifts.

Amen.

Katherine Crockett as the Pioneer Woman in *Appalachian Spring*

## 2. *Cave of the Heart*

*"For in other ways a woman*
*Is full of fear, defenseless, dreads the sight of cold*
*Steel; but, when once she is wronged in the*
*matter of love*
*    No other soul can hold so many thoughts of*
*blood."*
—Euripides, *Medea*

You will not have him. I gave him everything—even things I never should have sacrificed for him. My brother would interfere with your career? Gone. I will kill him. What do you need? I have it all, or I will get it and present it to you, and you will love me completely, perfectly, eternally. Nights I sat alone and waited for him to come home. The journey, the quest, of course, had to come first. I could wait. That was my offering to him. The minutes and hours were a perfect thing to please him, given without complaint.

My body was lovely. Firm breasts, high neck, proud smile, softness even I could see in mirrors, reflected in other faces. I listened to his stories, nodding encouragement, holding him in my arms with loving praise. Years did not matter, other lives blurred by; it was only we, we two.

And you think, now that I am older, not as shining, as sparkling as you, that he will leave me for you? No. We have a history, a past that defines each of us, binds us with steel. You will not have him. And if you try to take him, I will kill you, kill you effortlessly, without a thought.

*"It was everything to me to think well of one man,*
*And he, my own husband, has turned out wholly vile."*
—Euripides, *Medea*

We know this spurned woman, and we whisper about her betrayal when her husband abandons her for the second wife he flaunts as his trophy in some imagined contest. It's hard to know what to say. Do we invite her to dinner? Dare we speak of the iron bolts choking her breathing? Do we serve her by touching the wound or by looking anywhere but the gaping hole?

In the Greek myth, Medea, a sorceress, falls in love with Jason and employs her magical prowess to help him gain the Golden Fleece. Even though Medea sacrificed a child and her life for thankless Jason, he ultimately abandons her for a young princess. Enraged, Medea determines to kill the princess and murder her own two children. Jason will be left with nothing.

Artistic director Terese Capucilli reflects on the first time she danced Medea in *Cave of the Heart*. "*Cave* came late in my career. It was a role I was fearful of, one of the most challenging, since one is so completely exposed emotionally. There are four distinct voices that need to encompass the stage and somehow not focus in on each other. One must hold onto one's voice even when still." Here, Terese reflects the teachings of her great mentor, for Martha Graham spoke of "holding a movement, not daring to move, but moving." This is especially evident in Terese's powerful performance. Watch her crouched in the heart, in the small cave she fills. While Jason and his princess cavort, Medea in Terese's body is aware with every nerve, but no direct glance. This is active, energetic presence.

Terese goes on. "The stillness is intense and extremely difficult in this piece. The intensity of each character makes the work incredibly sparse. It must be clear."

In her overwhelming presence, it is.

As Terese grew in the role, she discovered that "all the ballets that led to Medea, all of Martha's work that I had done, was in Medea. I knew I had lived within her in many aspects of the repertoire. This gave me the confidence that I had matured through Martha's work."

*"I pray that I may see him, all their palace shattered*
*For the wrong they dare to do me without cause."*
—*Euripides, Medea*

Once Medea begins the dance of vengeance pictured here, in essence she is devouring her own innards. Terese continues, "That vengeance eats at you inside, and you will never be the same person again. You are completely consumed. For a woman, for anyone, to be possessed that way by jealousy and rage can move her even to murder her children. In dancing the role, one must reach out with one large voice. It has to be huge."

As Medea looks directly at the personification of her corrosive jealousy, here in a red, snakelike ribbon, she curves into an extended *attitude* coupled with powerful facial commands. Accompanying the moment are consuming shudders, all quite frightening.

At the dance's end, Medea slips into the metallic Noguchi garment of destiny, surrendering to her father the sun with a heroic thrust.

The stage is splashed with a blood-red background, and in the shimmering crystallization of fate, Medea escapes into eternity.

Nothing else matters anymore.

Nothing is left.

Thinking about Martha's pervasive influence, Terese believes that "one can discover oneself over and over again in the repertoire. You bring everything you have experienced or danced before. Each time you approach the role, you are able to find a different color. This is the genius of Martha."

Indeed, this perpetual well of meaning marks every great work of genius.

Terese Capucilli as Medea in *Cave of the Heart*

When Heidi Stoeckley, as the Chorus, watches Medea step furiously down her road of jealous anger, she at first covers her face, not wanting to watch. It is the horror that Kurtz saw in Joseph Conrad's *Heart of Darkness*. It is a snake wrapping itself in a sinuous strand through every fiber of our body, waiting for the perfect moment to clamp viciously and press all life out of us. The snake is there, always, but it is frightening to watch. Suspended in air in a straight jump up, the Chorus is our voice, our eyes, and our outstretched hands pleading for the anger to stop before something evil happens. Stop now. Don't go there. Heidi illuminates the thought process here.

"As the Chorus Woman, I behold all of the human heart, its ignored instincts and overlooked premonitions. I am the emotion that is shoved into the cave of the heart. As the voice of conscience to the other characters in this ballet, I am the source both of angst and of safety. All too often, from their perspective, to see me is to be afraid and to hear me is to feel my ache. I witness every detail of these characters' human existence, including their internal workings and external interactions. Because I hold such a personal and vulnerable place in their lives, I become a passageway, a secret trail guide to their happiness. Unfortunately, only the faithful and humble can light their way through my dark, cavernous trail. Medea, Jason, and the Princess struggle but fall prisoners to ignorance, emotion, and ego. Though I desire to be their gateway, they remain lost in the darkness of my cave."

The humiliated Medea has no fear, nothing else to lose. She winds her snakelike body between Jason and his princess; we stand with the choric figure as the village voice, embarrassed to watch. Don't choose this consuming rage.

"It is devastating to know certainly that a choice will bring destruction in someone we care for," Katherine Crockett observes. "This can be our spouse, our colleague, our student—anyone who cannot listen to warnings right now." Heidi Stoeckley feels her Chorus persona swoops into different heart caves through the dance—sometimes in Medea, later in the crushed hearts of the dead victims, and miraculously in our hearts at the end in a shimmer of rebirth and resurrection.

Sometimes, however, for the wronged victim, it is immolation, the release from reality that a destroyed soul desires. Let me fling myself with abandon on this flame—I no longer care.

*Heidi Stoeckley as the Chorus in Cave of the Heart*

As Jason parades his pretty princess for all, especially Medea, to see, we move upstage with the Chorus to embrace Medea. Let us hold you in our round arms and think of something else to do. Jason hardly seems worth the trouble, yet this blunt, arrogant man is the jewel for two women's crowns. When he tenderly holds his princess as if she would fly away, we see Medea despair and move to the next stage of her plan, one she paces out with cold, squared symmetry onstage. This cursed woman will die, and so will my children. She will never have them.

And the princess? Erica Dankmeyer knows her well. Her slight frame and light coloring suit the naiveté of a young girl who remains untouched by suffering.

"As royalty, I think she is used to having her own way, and when she finds Jason pursuing and possessing her, she proudly imagines that he is her destiny. If she senses the strife beneath their union, she does not acknowledge it. When I perch on Jason's shoulder, I must be light and carefree. This is difficult, as I am deadweight and we must draw our centers together in a quick recovery. I rarely look at Medea. Seeing her would erode my universe; her problems are her own, not mine."

True, except the smug princess dies, poisoned by Medea, who then drags her wrapped corpse onstage in a great dramatic moment. Unfolding the royal robe—now a shroud—Medea gives Jason his princess. A tricky moment onstage: the princess must unobtrusively allow Medea to drag her step by step, all the time pushing forward with one leg to help the process along.

With hands outstretched, fingers straining, Katherine as the Chorus throws her arms up in despair. No one will listen to her; her fate is failed witnessing.

The twin towers crumble. We move down a road of death, revenge, and shattered families. We watch, unhappily mute. Stop. Don't. And they cannot hear us. This is the agony of the choric voice in *Cave of the Heart*.

How far would we go to hate?

How far would we go to love?


Ask Jocasta.

Kenneth Topping as Jason and Erica Dankmeyer as the Princess in *Cave of the Heart*

## 3. *Night Journey*

The prophet Tiresias may have been blind, but he saw more horrible truths than Queen Jocasta could make herself face. The long-prophesied possibility that her infant son, left to perish in the rocky hills, had in fact lived had nagged at her for years after she agreed to wound and abandon him. Comfort came when she decided a baby with a ripped foot would fall asleep, not really understand pain, and die. Surely.

The other degree of peace came when she finally believed that she had done a generous, even loving, deed. Her boy, fated to kill his father and marry his mother, must be spared that sin. She paid the price of guilty torture gladly.

It was done.

Like lightning bolts piercing her heart, freezing her mind, came this afternoon's decisive message: Oedipus, her husband for over twenty years, father to their four children, was her lost son, her murdered babe.

It could not be true.

It was true.

In Sophocles' *Oedipus Rex,* Jocasta leaves stage to absorb the unthinkable. We never see her again, for she hangs herself in their bedroom.

Martha Graham goes into that bedroom and begins her night journey, touching things that there are no words for.

*The body says what words cannot.*
—*Martha Graham*

Artistic director Christine Dakin reflects on *Night Journey*: "Jocasta relives her past and sees her future through the lens of a single moment. I see the role very physically, feel in my body what Jocasta's body was feeling. How can a woman be at once mother, lover, and consort to the same man? The physical reality of that, the complexity, is stunning. The suckling moment is one of those fleeting moments that encapsulates the whole history. I am aware of him first as a man, perhaps consort, behind me, proud, formal. Then that spirals down around me and is transformed to the man as lover at my breast, that erotic shiver, only to change again as he is at my bosom as my child. I am holding the energy and power of that in my pelvis, legs, thighs."

Jocasta holds high a coiled rope when *Night Journey* commences; it serves as both the rope she will hang herself with and a symbol of the umbilical cord that ties Jocasta and Oedipus together in several ways. The rope tangles, but Tiresias cuts through it with his harsh truth. It is Tiresias who has the final heartbeats of the dance, pounding the stage with his staff.

Christine Dakin as Jocasta in *Night Journey*

Gary Galbraith as Tiresias swoops in a pitch turn, indicating with this circular revolution the cyclical nature of the prophet's bald truths. "Tiresias knows more than anyone, and he is reluctant to tell what he knows. Such horrible pain will follow. He has seen the effects of hard truths before in his life, and he takes no joy in revealing Oedipus' parentage. It's an enigmatic oxymoron: he sees nothing and knows all."

Tiresias is onstage before he actually moves or speaks, so when he does interact, he must make an onstage entrance. His staff is wisdom, time, and truth, beating away. Ostensibly aged, the vigor of his solo belies this fact and actually speaks to the living intensity of truth wherever it is found. Gary sees the "most poignant point of Tiresias' contribution to the ballet at the climactic moment. Upstage center with one leg on the bed, he must push Jocasta and Oedipus apart. He can't look at them. His story is larger than they are." Later, of course, Oedipus chooses to blind himself rather than see the world he has soiled and the children he has created.

The blurring of past and present marks much of Martha's works. There is only the present. Tiresias will not allow Jocasta to race to the peace of death until she fully relives her past.

Gary Galbraith as Tiresias in *Night Journey*

Various private moments surface in Jocasta's stream of consciousness. At one point, the husband and wife walk forward in a simple movement. They were committed and in love. The bed reminds Jocasta of deep pleasure, now guilty pleasure. She tries to hide under it, get away from it; she cannot. A wide split fall when Jocasta sits and crosses her knees, opening and closing her legs to her handsome young husband, moves them again to their bed.

Cloaks and veils serve to conceal and to invite Oedipus and Jocasta. At one point modestly covering her body, at another offering intimacy for lovers, the robe ultimately falls away when Oedipus rips the jeweled pin from her, blinding himself so he will never again see or desire her.

When Jocasta falls onto the marriage bed, abstractly conceived by Noguchi as the essence of a man and woman, the furies rush in. In her autobiography, Martha writes, "Those furies, the daughters of the night, are the terrors we all have. They are memories of things we dread to remember, things we wish to forget—the terrors. They must be recognized and lived through until they leave your mind."

Like the Chorus in *Cave of the Heart*, these Daughters of the Night stridently thrust themselves across stage with jagged attacks. They bear witness to the sins and pain. They fall backward, only to rise again in abrasive counterpoint and run off in twisted contortions.

*"Alas, alas, miserable!—that word alone can I say
unto thee, and no other word henceforth for ever.
   There beheld we the woman hanging by the neck
in a twisted noose of swinging cords.
   But he, when he saw her, with a dread, deep cry
of misery, loosed the halter whereby she hung."*
—*Sophocles, Oedipus Rex*

*Every dance is a kind of fever chart, a graph
of the heart.*
—*Martha Graham*

Christine Dakin as Jocasta and Kenneth Topping as Oedipus in *Night Journey*

## 4. *Phaedra*

Lust for a beautiful young man driven by a mature woman's perceived need. Not unknown today, it was the secret obsession of Phaedra in classical literature. She wanted her stepson, Hippolytus. Maybe the fog of "technicalities" lulled Phaedra into thinking the lust was not so bad. After all, he was not her son. No relation at all, really.

What was she missing with Theseus? Only a couple knows what really happens between them. And when he is gone, perhaps even dead, what strictures must a woman listen to? What are these unwritten rules, and how did we as a community of people come to follow them?

If we entrust our lives to pleasure and immediate gratification, the rules disappear.

In fact, Graham's dance allows us the time to reflect on questions often repressed. Why should I wait? Why should the vagaries of chance interfere with pleasure? Who am I hurting?

Of course, people do get hurt. Never mind that a petulant goddess, Aphrodite, herself rejected by Hippolytus, masterminded the whole sequence, maliciously stirring Phaedra to lust after her stepson. Here, the object of one-directional desire dies. Hippolytus is drawn only to the chaste goddess Artemis. Spurned Aphrodite puts retribution into movement; death and chaos follow. The returning husband is faced with a lost, romantically tortured wife. Does he know why this happened?

Traditionally, Phaedra commits suicide after shocking Hippolytus with her advances, causing him to leave home. She composes a letter to be read after her death, accusing her stepson of rape. Martha relishes the moment onstage. Phaedra reenacts the purported perfidy for the appalled Theseus. In so doing, she can live out her suppressed sexual gratification.

Kenneth Topping as Theseus, Christine Dakin as Phaedra, and Tadej Brdnik as Hippolytus in *Phaedra*

Unlike Jocasta or Medea, Phaedra knowingly wreaks havoc on innocents. Like both of these tragic heroines, Phaedra kills herself rather than face the truth and live with it. She is ashamed of these uncontrollable urges and of her failure to overcome passion with reason. She constructs her own labyrinth when she succumbs to what Graham described as the "expressive instant of obsession by desire—over which there is no control or ease until death."

In Racine's version of *Phaedra*, she dies with the word *purity* on her lips, praying to the god of death, for she longed to be no more. Christine Dakin contracts her body in passionate power as Phaedra. "How dark is she? How possessed is her mind and body? She is on a desperate and single-minded quest, even as her internal conflict is embodied in her muscles, one set restricting another as she twists in different directions."

Miki Orihara has little sympathy for Phaedra. "I am the goddess Aphrodite, and I have made all the mischief happen. I don't like Phaedra and want to hurt her. She deserves to suffer. My flying ribbon is fate, whims, my mood at the moment. I try to say this with quick, decisive movements, with my breath intakes. My breathing technique here perfectly illustrates Martha's focus on contraction and release. Those are the two elements of our life and dance. We breathe in and out. That is the basis for contraction and release. Yuriko always said contraction is not a shape; it is an emotion turning into motion. If you feel one way, your body makes a certain shape—that becomes the shape of your individual contraction. For me, even in the tiniest of motions in my body, I have contraction. That must be released, either slowly or quickly, for without release there is no contraction. Of course, the release can simply be the neutral shape of our body, not just high arch or high lift."

Miki Orihara as Aphrodite in *Phaedra*

This was no ancient myth to Martha. In her handwritten notebooks is a side note in her arched penmanship:

*It happened*
*once upon a time—*
*It happens——*
*Every day———*

From Martha Graham's Journals:

*It is the time of the drought with Phaedra—*
*It is the time of the search of the blood for a*
*kindred pulse—*
*It is the desperate time when the need is for renewal,*
*the blessed rain*
*And the feeling of fertility again.*

Christine Dakin as Phaedra in *Phaedra*

## 5. *Errand into the Maze*

In the Greek myth of Ariadne and Theseus, the Minotaur—half man and half bull—rules from an impenetrable labyrinth constructed by the master architect Daedalus. He gives Minos' daughter, Ariadne, a ball of string with which to trace her steps and ensure escape should she venture into the labyrinth. In fact, Ariadne is half-sister to the beast; he is a frightening part of herself.

Why does she enter the maze? There is the mystery of our subconscious desires, and the lure is irresistible. Martha explained, "This dance has a special significance for me because it expresses the conquering of fear in my life; fear of the unknown, fear of something not quite recognizable."

No place is safe. Trapped in the maze, Ariadne is sure there is a way out. She can think and follow a plan. Stepping purposefully back and forth over the thick white rope, the rope that should lead to light and freedom, Ariadne makes no progress and, even worse, hears something.

Something is out there.

*If I am very good and very quiet, maybe it will miss me and just go away.*

A familiar, desperate hope for all of us, trying to believe we can escape the threat in the dark. Ultimately, schemes do not succeed, and eventually we must face our monsters.

Miki Orihara senses the Minotaur is there before she sees him, and her choreographic choices reflect the awesome pull of the creature. She moves into her body to find the one remaining safe place. She must be calm to fight back; she garners her energy. As our own fears can totally absorb us, threatening paralysis, Miki finds no rest and is in constant movement until the dance ends.

Is the Minotaur outside of us? Inside? Is he the outsider we wholly reject? The lover who does not know how to love?

We watch the dance unfold and move into our own mazes.

Gary Galbraith as the Minotaur and Elizabeth Auclair as Ariadne in *Errand into the Maze*

The beast, misshapen, awkward, bound by his own terrible yoke, knows only gross fear and confrontation. In the face of this, the very human Ariadne has no voice. The beast comes closer and blocks any way out. He becomes the whole of it.

For Miki, "I feel differently about the Minotaur with each partner. Our bodies determine our psychological connection and the degree to which I can protect myself and not lose my identity. In a sad way, the Minotaur could be the one who wants to connect, to be with you but does not know how."

But what does the Minotaur think? Whitney V. Hunter knows, for he lives the role intensely. From the first entrance when the beast fiercely stomps his presence, balancing precariously on one leg, this force must be acknowledged.

Whitney says, "I watch her from offstage. So really our interaction begins in those shadows. I see her maneuvering, planning, and I want to destroy her. I will not go away. To arrive larger than I am and awe her with fear, I make my entrance with a run timed to stop before I get to the spot in front of her. He knows exactly how many steps it is to his prey. This wild bull/man of total energy owns the ground, the earth."

Here is Graham sensibility blended with emotional reality, always her goal. Whitney says, "I grind deep into the ground with pelvic thrusts, pulling my hips back and getting my leg out in an enormously powerful thrust. I drop from the sky, so to speak." Clearly, the moment affects the audience kinesthetically.

"I am," he grins, "her worst nightmare. Times ten!"

With no short-term memory, he bounds back in all three confrontations, stronger, fiercer each time. In his second entrance, for example, he arrives downstage. She has a direct view of him on a shallow diagonal from the bone window, and he paces up and down the diagonal to her.

"Remember that dark alley? Here I am again."

Alessandra Prosperi notes that in dancing this role, "I am determined and will not be denied. At the same time, I realize how vulnerable we can be. In this case, I've decided to overcome my own fears, but it takes the length of the ballet to make it happen. It is not until the third entrance of the Minotaur that I finally defeat him. Ariadne turns to face him, beginning to think that she is stronger than she thought. 'I will do this thing.' In the course of the dance, I really come into my own physically, emotionally, intellectually. It is a birth of power."

One of the most electric moments in the piece comes when Ariadne is on the floor rolling away from the bone. Whitney thinks she is "like a dog trapped by an invisible electronic fence. Every time my foot comes down on either side of her, I remind her that I own this space. Don't think about moving." He shifts at the base of his spine in a deep spiral, in deep, extreme twists in a cruel parody of Ariadne's own rope march earlier. All this ferocity must be conveyed while moving with head and mouth gear. Eventually the Minotaur's bone and horns become second nature to the performer so encumbered. Whitney moves as if they are not even there. "Bone? What bone?" he laughs. "Actually, the horns are very light."

Whitney V. Hunter as the Minotaur in *Errand into the Maze*

In a last desperate scream to the gods, Ariadne fights back, jumping onto the Minotaur and defeating him. She now owns this space, which she fills with light, freedom, and joy. Standing in a doorframe of whitened bones, she lingers where she has been and knows that she can go on. Her composed body and steady gaze epitomize the human soul that faced the worst and survived.

Fang-Yi Sheu dances this role with a furious intensity. Her extreme leg extension is the objective realization of every scrap of determination and courage she bears for Ariadne. "By the end of this dance, I can look around me in a new part of my soul, and the future is full of possibilities. There is nothing I cannot do!"

A gentle and thoughtful man offstage, Whitney philosophically sets this dance in a special perspective.

"I think courage comes in narrow bits of time and space. I think about this when I remember 9/11. The people on the higher floors thought that there was no other option for saving themselves except to jump. They faced fire. They were Ariadne. For them, for all of us, the only way we can survive is if we face this 'monster' and devour him. As an artist, I have to keep these images before me, to help me get beyond technical difficulties and into a place of modern relevance."

In both *Errand into the Maze* and in *Circe*, Martha celebrates the triumph of humanity. Ariadne and Ulysses bravely face down demonic fears and temptations.

They embrace the dance of life.

Fang-Yi Sheu as Ariadne in *Errand into the Maze*

# 6. Circe

Circe follows part of Ulysses' homeward journey after the Trojan War. His wife, Penelope, is waiting for him; so is his son. Ulysses loved Penelope so much that one post of their wedding bed was a tree whose spidery tendrils dug ever deeper into the earth as the years of their marriage passed. It was a good marriage. But he has been away twenty years, and the journey home has been fraught with detours. It has been exhausting.

The enticing calls of mermaids and beautiful creatures from an enchanted island waft over Ulysses at his weakest moment. Of course, tempting calls to forbidden pleasures entice us most when we are weakest. Why not visit those slender arms? How can a little pleasure, a little night music, hurt?

Circe rules this exotic island and holds nothing back. A whirl of passionate red, she is sex, pleasure. Now. Here. Come to me. And he wants her.

Circe knows this. Katherine Crockett, here in a provocative arabesque, swirls her red gown almost like perfume whose essence is part of her being. "I wrap the fabric around him in animal lust. It is every part of me, the concrete expression of my allure. The gown is her heat, her power to enchant him, first perhaps as a game, but then with true desire to possess him in every way. I studied this myth to help construct my role as Circe. Her father is Helios, the sun, so the sun itself must be in her. Ulysses may be imagining her or remembering the first moment he saw her, but she is on a cloud, shimmering light down on him. Within all of this, Christine's [Dakin] direction allowed me many ways to make the role my own, to believe in my own interpretation."

## Tadej Brdnik as Ulysses

Ulysses tied himself to the mast of his ship so he could not mislead his men and direct them to dangerous liaisons. Graham zooms in on the hero as he comes close to Circe's island, clearly an unnecessary stop. Sensing danger, his loyal helmsman sets himself as sentinel on his master's soul and implores him not to leave his ship. As Ulysses, Tadej Brdnik dances the role torn apart about what to do.

"Life is full of choices. Ulysses knows the facts but is beyond them. He is living on some other, deeper level of raw desire."

Martha Graham knew that our deepest self is not rational or balanced, but lives in the moment of passion. Knowledge and facts go only so far. Tadej muses, "Ulysses does not know who he is. Is he this hero everyone calls him? To follow temptations means leaving part of himself behind, and that might not be a bad thing."

It is always this wrenching moment that intrigues Graham. Now. Whatever I do next means I will be different, new somehow. Shall I?

Tadej continues. "As I dance more of her roles, as I mature and my own life grows, I find more of myself exposed on stage. Am I dancing my life? Does the dance, who I am onstage, affect my life? Where is the wall? Where is my real life?"

Indeed, Martha reflected on this phenomenon herself.

"The sweep of life catches up the mere personality of the performer, and while the individual (the undivided one) becomes greater, the personal becomes less personal."

Katherine Crockett as Circe in *Circe*

Kenneth Topping as Ulysses with Whitney V. Hunter, Martin Lofsnes, Christophe Jeannot, and Maurizio Nardi in *Circe*

Tadej works this dilemma out as he dances. "He thinks, 'Do I go on, go home? Do I cross the water to this island?' So he leaves the boat and goes to her. The consequences are not so terrible. Ulysses sees his men enchanted by this witch, and in their animal faces he still sees his men. They are in there somewhere."

Perhaps to distract him, the animals move constantly, and the Deer, Goat, Lion, and Snake all seem content. They are not human, but they are not in agony. The Snake insinuates a special affinity for Circe, as he was the first to fall to her enchantment. Martin Lofsnes enjoys being this knowing creature. "He slides up and down slowly, sexually, gracefully and lingers close to Circe. Definitely the leader!"

### Christophe Jeannot as the Deer

"As the Deer, I am very angular, sharp. I feed off the energy of the other dancers/animals. The Snake, who I think is Circe's favorite, is really in charge. She sends him out as her disciple, and we all sort of acknowledge his position with our body deference. He was the first animal she charmed, so he is special to her. I dance this part, too, and then I feel this in my dominance. And let me just tell you: I'm really afraid of snakes!

"The Deer, though, is not some timid animal. I love my antlers and put them forward for everyone to see. It is a joy to be the Deer!

"Now, Ulysses can be beaten. I think so. But he is very intelligent. I just think he is very vulnerable right now—too bad for him—as he passes our island. Our island. I am here to do my job. I am completely enchanted by Circe, and I have absolutely no questions. Send me! I am efficient. I am hers.

"And you must know this, yes? In this dance of Martha's, the men dominate!"

### Maurizio Nardi as the Goat

"You would not think there is much room for Martha's technique in this animal, but there is. He is very angular. So the contraction and the release must be very sharp. We must not confuse my angularity with the Deer, who prances more. My arms must always be out for my horns. The Goat is constantly wary, alert. Martha's technique here is a very natural illumination of this quick, quick animal. I had a lot of fun being the Goat. We were Circe's fingers, reaching out to pick Ulysses up for her. After all, the piece is about seduction. The Goat is very sexy! He swerves from his groin; he shakes his testicles, strong pulls down to the ground. He jumps often, and I try to keep the energy clean, high and 'in' rather than 'out.'"

The animals charm, but not enough.

## Gary Galbraith as the Helmsman

At crucial junctures, Ulysses gets advice from his loyal helmsman. Gary Galbraith performs the role as Ulysses' alter ego, and every muscle in Gary's body cries out, "No! Do not go there." Sensing evil and alert to his ability to protect his leader, the Helmsman takes his responsibility seriously.

Gary observes, "The Helmsman has seen what happened to his shipmates. They are now enchanted and no longer human. They were obstacles in Circe's way for the main event—Ulysses. Maybe she wants him so much because she may not be able to have him.

I know more than Ulysses at this point, and I want to save him. When my arms stretch out over him, I feel I am part of him, the responsible man who must get us all home. Here he must wrench himself to the ground, up again, to find the place he belongs. In Circe's arms, it becomes easier to submit. Will he remain a man, at least the man he thought he was?"

Anxious but deferential, the Helmsman must watch helplessly. Gary allows this grave intuition to inform his body at every moment of the ballet. "I feel stillness, knowledge amidst movement. Circe and her creatures never stop moving. It is in my solid stillness that my angst speaks. I am a powerful observer, and the eye of the audience, I hope, lingers with me. The stillness is not passive; it is wisdom."

This knowing witness is crucial to many Graham works. The Attendant in *Herodiade*, Tiresias in *Night Journey*, the Chorus in *Cave of the Heart* each bear the loving insight they absolutely believe will protect someone they care for.

Parents watch teenagers drive off into the night with friends who may drink or take drugs. Don't go. Please, please don't. Arrogance in business ventures, ruling nations, and waging wars takes our breath away, for we can taste coming disaster. Do not go there! This way there be dragons. Stop before it is too late. You are going to drown all of us!

But the ship sails on.

Ulysses is not a god; he is human. His urge to be enveloped in Circe's exciting, voluminous cloak makes this clear. When he finally sails away from the island, his longing look back, his arching neck and shoulders tensing even as he moves across the wine dark sea to Penelope mark him as a real person.

Joseph Campbell wrote, "All stories are the same story." They are. That one story is the hero's journey to face the worst dangers life can spin, do one's best, and then go home. It is what we do every day. We face the challenges, making decisions we did not know yesterday that we would have to make today.

We do this. And why? So we can return to that safe place of joy and satisfaction where we feel complete.

Call it home.

Tadej Brdnik as Ulysses and Gary Galbraith as the Helmsman in *Circe*

## 7. Dark Meadow

From the beginning of time we have found satisfaction in things done in ritual, things speaking of the past. In some deep sense we believe we can come to a well of healing at our primal source.

In her notes preparatory to this ballet, Martha Graham quotes St. Augustine: "I will come to the fields and spacious palaces of my memory."

In the work, three central figures roam this spacious palace of memory: One Who Seeks, He Who Summons, and She of the Earth. The very titles raise the figures to archetypal status.

In this complicated space dotted with four symbolic Noguchi creations, one hopes for a directional thread. It is here. While She Who Seeks does just that, and rather anxiously, sprightly couples spring up and just fall in love, or lust, fool around, and generally enjoy life. They move in a dreamy symmetry in lyrical love duets, moving slowly in some challenging floor movements. In virtuoso moves for the ensemble, the men must support the full weight of crouched women on their chests, approaching and retreating on their knees. The subtext to allow love to have its way may be the greatest message in this early dance of Martha's, a thought echoed later in the frank fun of *Satyric Festival Song* and the deliciously silly *Maple Leaf Rag*. Dance! Just that! Don't think all the time! Lighten up! See this brown dirt? The flowers are going to bloom soon.

Christine Dakin as She Who Seeks in *Dark Meadow*

And bloom they do, as She of the Earth guides the seeker into full womanhood, away from arid stones and Plato's malevolent goddess Ate, who lures to sin, even past the sexual ferocity of He Who Summons, into the light of flowers and colors that transform the rocky landscape. She Who Seeks encounters erotic love here, and in her solitary stance at the close she has moved beyond its call. She awaits what is to come on every level. Katherine Crockett as She of the Earth is a tender guide. "I want to bring the seeker through a ritual happening right now to help her become the woman she was meant to be. At the end of the ballet I guide her in an angular, tightly restricted walk, with frontal presentation and perspective that reminds me of Egyptian hieroglyphics and tomb paintings. It is not religious, but it is sexual, primal, primitive life force."

The woman may be approaching self-awareness on many levels. Martha's good friend and brilliant choreographer Agnes de Mille thought the work reflected Martha's own artistic odyssey and that she dances through a wasteland, eschewing all pleasure in sacrifice to her art. However, this wasteland comes to life, and Noguchi posts sprout leaves and greenery, blessed by She of the Ground.

*To everything there is a season, and a time to every purpose under heaven:*
*A time to weep, and a time to laugh;*
*A time to mourn, and a time to dance.*
*—Ecclesiastes*

Katherine Crockett as She of the Ground in *Dark Meadow*

## 8. *Embattled Garden*

Eve, languidly combing her hair, clearly bored and with no plans for lunch, casts her eyes around the garden, hoping for . . . something. Adam is unconcerned; their days are routine now.

The malicious serpent and his willing partner, Lilith, ooze into the garden. The serpent, the other, the Stranger, bites Eve on the neck directly, viciously, without prelude. Lilith, with some rights of territory here as Adam's first wife, waits to see what will happen next.

It seems we all crave change, want more, and if some impulses do damage, well . . .

When Miki Orihara comes to her performance as Eve in *Embattled Garden*, she invests the woman with prescience, a creature attuned to nuances around her. Before the serpent enters, Miki knows he is there, knows something is wrong and also that somehow she is the cause of the problem. The serpent's bite, while alarming, is exciting as well. Miki tries to stare down Lilith, to ponder her strange attraction to the Stranger, and to consider how she feels about Adam.

"This crisis comes too fast for Eve," Miki notes. "I do not think Eve loves Adam at the beginning of the dance. When she sees she could lose him to Lilith, her desire is renewed." They come together, turn their backs on each other, and stew.

"When Eve turns to Adam again, she is making a conscious choice and she commits to go on," Miki observes.

Tadej Brdnik as Adam and Miki Orihara as Eve in *Embattled Garden*

Elizabeth Auclair, Lilith in her yellow dress, wants to cause trouble, and her machinations are supported by the Stranger, Christophe Jeannot. Lilith snaps her fan faster and faster in irritation as she sees her scheme unravel. Adam shifts back and forth between Lilith, Eve, and the Stranger and seems to be everywhere at once. David Zurak remarks that Adam's "long extensions thrusting up off the garden floor with fast pulls down followed by returns upward call for use of the whole body. One cannot overly indulge these deep pulls and returns or it becomes cliché Graham. Restraint is called for."

Christophe Jeannot as the Stranger, Tadej Brdnik as Adam, and Elizabeth Auclair as Lilith in *Embattled Garden*

*Embattled Garden* speaks to our fickleness, our reluctance to lose what we have, a reluctance driven by the sometimes difficult decision just to stay where we are.

What will I gain?

What will I lose?

Is it worth it?

Miki lives in Eve's skin and likes her. She dances Eve as the flip side of another woman, Ariadne of *Errand into the Maze*. As a counter to Eve, who opts for the status quo, even if it has become ordinary, Ariadne, who appears to have lost all choice in an entrapping maze, fights back.

Tadej Brdnik as Adam and Miki Orihara as Eve in *Embattled Garden*

*The greatest joys of mankind*
*are within us*
*and within our reach.*
—*Seneca*

Miki Orihara as Eve in *Embattled Garden*

## 9. *Primitive Mysteries*

Within every woman rests the potential for new life. As rich as the earth itself, woman feeds life with her body, transforming herself to gift and giver, exemplifying the essential grace and beauty of flesh. In this body, somewhere, roams the soul, looking for its home, its mother. It is a wonderfully ordinary mystery. In *Primitive Mysteries*, Graham sifts through the formal gestures of ritual, the honed, repeated movements which by their very repetition lend weight and meaning to our feeble attempts to visualize divinity.

We use what we have: our bodies, sound, rhythm, silence, space, and stillness. Several times in this ballet, Martha sanctifies space by placing one toe on the floor and letting the foot fall in place. Here.

This moment. All is holy. In its tender simplicity, this smallest of dance movements speaks for all of dance. One toe, one bare foot, and wood. This work is timed to match heartbeats, calm breathing, and the constancy of life. It lifts the soul higher than it thought it could go. The viewer has the chance to experience grace.

Here and in *El Penitente*, Martha devotes time to Mary, the mother of Christ and a universal archetype of woman and mother. The medieval Christian raised Mary to cult status, erecting magnificent cathedrals to her—Notre Dame de Paris, Notre Dame de Chartres, and so many more. In the dark, empty spaces of those cathedrals, prayers float to heaven, gently presented to a son by his mother. Surely those prayers would be heard.

But beneath the goddess rites linking mother to eternity is the true story every mother lives.

Her child is born, and after the tenderest nurturing he leaves, never to come home in the same way. The mother's heart yearns for that babe even as she proudly witnesses his mature days.

And pain comes. Pain for him is worse than any personal anguish. She sees him unloved, rejected, disappointed, and she is unable to help. And sometimes, incredibly, he dies as she watches. So it has been forever, and so it was for Mary.

Elizabeth Auclair as the Virgin in *Primitive Mysteries*

The celebration and mourning inherent in motherhood is most appropriately noted by other women. In *Primitive Mysteries*, they form the circles of joy and woe, lending both witness and support.

Under the Graham hand, women enter as sacred acolytes, reverently spacing themselves in anticipation of Mary's entrance. In this simply told story, Martha absorbs the spareness of the New Mexico she so loved, moving within the Hispanic-Indian frame of ceremonies honoring the Blessed Virgin. The broken rhythms that become prayer propel each section of the ballet ritual to its conclusion. Created in 1931, *Primitive Mysteries* is a precursor to *El Penitente*, where the Graham eye centers on Christ.

The dance brings one attending woman home. Brenda Nieto speaks.

"I am from Mexico. When I wear this blue dress and walk onstage with all the other women, I feel I am in a dream. For me, it is to touch the true Virgin Mary. I have to open all of my mind and body to feel everyone—the women before me, the women behind me. I feel them and all the women of my life as one.

"In Mexico, the people come to Mary to ask favors. Sometimes they come to special *iglesias*, or shrines, on their knees, in the dust. They come to beg. So when we move in our circles, I think that every dancer is a woman, too, one who has needs, one who asks forgiveness, for a blessing. Everyone comes with a full heart. Some need. Some say thank you. It is a prayer."

*Hail Mary, full of grace*
*The Lord is with thee*
*Blessed art thou among women*

Mary enters and is both with these women, blessing them with her presence, yet mystically above them. A young and vulnerable Mary walks seriously down the aisle of attending women. Hands prayerfully clasped, she is separate but somehow one of these women. She walks with them. "I feel potential and mystery as I walk," Elizabeth reveals. "Both qualities are with me all the time."

She wears a layered organdy dress with semi-detached petal cap sleeves. Luminously white, it floats. Clean to the touch, it feels light and invites internal movement within its hidden scooping layers. Ingeniously simple, the gown itself is a virginal voice.

The chorus of women also moves in gowns that physically manifest their symbolic standing. How moving to watch thirteen women in blue jersey dresses that fall easily to the floor but are caught by girlish white ruffles. They are bells. They ring and swing silently onstage, and their silence becomes sound. The skirts offer a sobering weight to the proceedings, but swing gently, as young girls will.

And the women bow to Mary.

With sudden reversals and plunges into knee bends, the women venerate the Virgin in a dramatic, climactic bow. Encircling Mary with their arms, they even cradle her as she collapses into their waiting arms. As danced by Elizabeth Auclair, Mary is very aware of all these textures. Her body must be perfectly aligned to the waiting arms of the attendants, a moment not without tension, and she must just let go. Her body moves down, ready to rise again—a quintessential Graham technique working

Christine Dakin (right) as the Virgin with Jennifer Conley in *Primitive Mysteries*

artistically and metaphorically. "Mary is vulnerable and open at that moment," Elizabeth observes. "The pelvic strength to rise is there, waiting."

In the women's arms, Mary does not see that their hands really form a crown of flowers above her head. A more bitter crown of thorns is ahead. They must leave her, and they do so silently two more times. They depart slowly, deliberately, preparing for what is to come.

### Mater Dolorosa

"Mary has an air of unquestioning acceptance. As Mary, I know I am meant to be here and do this. There is no point bemoaning the misery. Freedom comes in acceptance of this plan. Martha always cues into the cyclical nature of all living things, including our emotional life. Nothing stays the same. When the worst is over, it can only get better. So all of this was for something very good. Mary knows."

It is just this prescient interpretation of a role that defines a Graham dancer of Elizabeth's caliber. Martha spoke often of the "interior landscape of emotion" and challenges her dancers and audiences to explore that bleak reality with her. There is a strange comfort in ritual. The pageant nature of this dance allows one to view the drama as one seen before but felt anew each time. We know the end of the story, but the journey still intrigues.

As Mary drags her body toward the crucifixion of her son, even to move her legs is excruciating. Legs lock, move haltingly forward and back, and step by step she comes beneath the cross.

Christine Dakin takes us into Mary's body and soul and moves Mary beyond religious resonance to universal spirit. "She reflects eternal cycles of youth, maturity, and death with innocence, knowledge, transformation—the oneness of joy and sorrow, present, past, and future. She focuses 'beyond' in the theater, and we understand her gaze simultaneously as a private act and public acknowledgment—private pain and public duty. She slows time to a standstill as she agonizingly, slowly, lets her arms fall, bit by bit. She is alone, and she is totally among us." The negative open space around Mary is full. She is enveloped in silence used as sound. She leaves as she came, to repeat the cycle and continue her journey.

### Hosannah

Ultimately, peace and light prevail and Mary, Queen of Heaven, takes as her throne the simple space in a circle of thirteen women as her jewels. On the floor in a Buddha pose, she extends one hand upward to receive daily graces and lets the other hand open. She is ready to accept divine wisdom and send it on a flowing current to those who wait. Us.

The women leave the stage as they came: bare feet pad on the ground in heartbeats.

Amen.

Christine Dakin as the Virgin in *Primitive Mysteries*

## 10. *El Penitente*

In *El Penitente* the story of the Christ rests in the hands of a troupe of street players. The voice of every man, the jugglers and tricksters try to catch the audience's eyes and hearts. They are the acrobats of God, pulling stories from air and memory, bringing them to life right before our eyes.

In the spirit of Hispanic folk rituals, *El Penitente* is like a mystery play based on biblical stories. The title refers to the sect of Penitents of the American Southwest who seek physical penance as a means of self-purification from sin.

The dance centers on the self-flagellating Penitent, the Christ figure, and Mary in tripartite personae as Virgin, Magdalene, and Mother. Here, Christ's work is not finished, not even on the cross. Mary, whom we watched begin her own pilgrimage to this pace in *Primitive Mysteries*, is here. So is Mary Magdalene, the temptress, but she also seems to be Eve.

Looming above everyone is Jesus Christ. In this role, Maurizio Nardi uses his body carefully, slowly, to allow his masked head to hover over those at his feet. Encumbered by a large Noguchi mask, Christ is a remote but supportive presence. The shadow cast is both literal and divine. Christ does not speak, but his compassionate body tells all. "If I move too quickly, the figure would be comic. He must be felt as divine, but still able to allow for human error and forgive."

Maurizio also inhabits the revivalist preacher in *Appalachian Spring* and draws viable parallels. "The preacher has experienced life differently from those he counsels. He comes to judge and support at the same time. So does the suffering Christ here."

The Penitent, Tadej Brdnik, writhes across stage moving into the arched twists of a man beating himself with a rope. "Here, I must move into the responsive reaction before the rope actually strikes so that the action is pulled from me." Later in the series of ten sequences, the Penitent hauls a cart of metaphorical sin and sorrow behind him, and as he absorbs his sinfulness, he moves toward atonement even to the point of becoming another Christ carrying his own cross. Mary, now as mother, curves her body in a parallel gesture of suffering to walk with her son, with all sinners.

Tadej Brdnik as the Penitent in *El Penitente*

The young virgin, Alessandra Prosperi, carries a bit of heavenly blue sky with her in a curved halo. She personifies the Navajo chant that inspired Martha:

*Beauty lies before me,*
*beauty lies to the right of me,*
*beauty lies to the left of me.*
*I walk in beauty.*
*I am beauty.*

Alessandra suggests that she may not even be there literally as this young Mary. "I think I am the comforting sky, I am heaven, I am all that is light and fresh. I stretch and pull my torso up like a cloud. Later, my role changes in a very short transition. This dance moves very quickly from spot to spot, and our characters are different within seconds.

"The flirting woman is Eve. She offers a juicy, red apple, the apple we all recall from the story in the Garden of Eden, but it may be me, myself, inside and out. Want some? Come on! The twisted turns when the apple is on my hips says all that.

"The Magdalene figure appears in the Crucifixion segment, comforting the penitent, showing her compassion. *El Penitente* really has lighthearted moments, especially if we compare it to the more dramatic Graham works. The challenge for me is to portray all the different figures with their diversity, complexity, and beauty. I am never offstage. I am either on or hiding behind the set, then moving the cart, the mask, the veils—everything has to be perfect. It can be cumbersome to worry about objects as well as characterization, but I love it. In this ballet, everything happens right here and now, and Martha wanted the audience to experience this as live theater, actually becoming part of the ritual onstage."

Alessandra's insights match with the fact that early Graham audiences were unused to abstract modern dance, coming from theatrical experiences grounded in vaudeville, musicals replete with quickly changing acts.

Alessandra Prosperi as Mary in *El Penitente*

Martin Lofsnes uses his long, lean body to good effect as the Christ. "This divine being is complex. When I enter using long, spare steps squaring off space in stark, unembellished movements, I *am* law. The law is linear, square. Marking off both time and space makes sense. The whole role tells me to be true to the choreography because every movement will read. One of the tenderest moments for me is the arm extensions to the Penitent. He reaches up to me, I reach down to him, but we never quite meet. It's a sequence of pleading and forgiveness.

"This Christ is removed from the human realm by the mask. In technical terms, it's horrendous, making it very difficult to use any angle other than straight frontal. You can't adopt various angles the way you can with your face. It is challenging to try to give it life—almost like puppetry. The slightest tip or tilt gives a reading. I've spent a lot of time in front of a mirror trying to do more with the mask, but I can hardly see out of it. It's held on by a mouthpiece, so my clenched teeth are the control. Dancing with props really is an art unto itself. I have watched this dance executed by others in the company for many years. Those hours spent offstage watching were essential to making the piece my own."

Serious thought. Meditative suggestions. When the familiar sequence of sin, penance, and forgiveness is complete, what comes next? Move, be alive, celebrate . . . dance! The performers cast aside the dark rites and let their bodies move and breathe.

Life goes on.

Tadej Brdnik as the Penitent, Martin Lofsnes as Christ Figure, and Elizabeth Auclair as Mary in *El Penitente*

## II. *Deep Song*

In her canon of solos, *Deep Song* (1937) and *Lamentation* (1930) emerge as crucial works for Martha Graham. In both pieces she explores the depths of personal anguish. Provoked by the Spanish Civil War, *Deep Song* is abstract, a dance without linear narrative. Criticized in 1937 for its polemic point of view, *Deep Song* continues to breathe with truth as mothers' sons still die and kill other women's sons. In its archetypal tone, the dance goes where the soul has always traveled. One woman writhes in agony on a wooden bench, and we watch.

For Alessandra Prosperi, the bench "is a grave where I mourn and finally come back to life. This is a woman—every woman. Who has died? Is it her son, her brother, her husband? Is he really dead or just away? I must work with this pain. I keep the pain focused to the context of war. This is fresh agony, not for one dead a long time. When I rock from side to side, I think of the pain of the Madonna, of Jesus. It is very personal. I know that I move as a real woman, a human being going through this. The bench itself anchors me, pulling me in as much as I, at times, reject it."

Martha really loved the Picasso painting *Guernica*, and many images from this work appear in the ballet—the tortured face of a woman, arms and hands extending upward.

"This work can be compared to *Lamentation*. I think it is an extension of *Lamentation*. While *Lamentation* is the pain itself in visual form, *Deep Song* personifies this pain and places it in the heart and body of a real woman."

Alessandra has come to own this work. "In shaping this piece, I struggled to find my true freedom of spirit. This comes after coming into control of every single step and then becoming comfortable with dancing 'on the edge' with live music. I feel liberated. I am not trying to be any other dancer or Martha. I must own and control the steps before I can add my own interpretation. In *Deep Song*, I do."

Alessandra has devoted herself to Martha's works since 1987 and is one of the current company personally selected by Graham to dance. "In 1986, Martha came to Florence and I was a young ballet dancer there. Unfortunately, I did not know who she was. We took auditions with her, and I was chosen for a repertory workshop taught by Yuriko. So I began this 'Graham experience.' My body screamed! For days, I could not walk, could not have a massage. But it became natural for me, and finally we did a presentation dance for Martha. The performance was in front of a palace, and I remember being presented to this old woman seated like a queen, reaching out her long hand to me, telling me sweet things. When I was offered the scholarship to come to New York to the Graham School, I knew I had to go. I left my family, my friends, my country for it.

"She opened my life, changed everything. To dance one of her great solos sends me into her soul and mine. I will never leave."

# 12. *Lamentation*

*Lamentation*, the earlier piece, addresses even more abstract emotion and delves into the essence of pain itself, of deep primal screams. The sorrow wraps itself around the woman's body, encasing her in a fabric tube that becomes a second skin. The sorrow itself overwhelms the dancer as she casts eyes desperately upward, seeking a way out. There is none. Clenched fists beat at the heart, and every part of the body takes lightning hits of pain. Hanging contractions and quivering thrusts personify torment. Finally, it becomes her own, and she must find a way to live within its tentacles. The arched back, stretches in torso, and even in the feet all work in agonized wrenching to articulate ultimate loss. And so it is. The more we resist, the more we are trapped.

These ballets dip into the collective Jungian unconscious that we share. We do not know why this all seems so familiar. It just is. We are witnessing our blood memory.

Graham presents the contemporary audience with an objective correlative as defined by T. S. Eliot. The poet and literary critic knew that an audience faced with stark anguish as naked as those facing devastating loss sees not an art object but the actual emotion itself. Unfolding before us, these gestures, movements, facial compositions immediately evoke the emotion. For a brief moment we move neither forward nor backward. The world may be moving, but we are at its still center.

Both solos are pain incarnate, and to watch them is to watch ourselves. This is dance.

## 13. *Herodiade*

After dancing erotically for her stepfather, Herod, in honor of his birthday, Salome granted her mother's request and asked for the head of John the Baptist, who had denounced her mother's marriage. Beyond the biblical context, the ballet *Herodiade* looks into the soul of any woman facing loss and change powerlessly.

Martha Graham's artistic passions drove her into a small, private world. Conscious choices forged a life explored onstage metaphorically but lived in private pain. Choosing to be an artist meant other doors closed for her. She remained childless, the love of her life was ephemeral, and gradually she secluded herself from even her close friends and faced her final years alone rather than in company. She knew she was not like other women but was powerless to resist the forces that overtook her.

It is this woman we see onstage, one whose total and linear commitment to her life now surprises her with whatever is next. A special, superior woman, she commands respect and accepts obeisance as her due. Because she has risen above so many others, she can let them bow to her; therefore, she can never collapse in their arms for tender mercies.

Things are changing here. There is little choice. Noguchi's bonelike mirror reflects this person at this moment. She sees her body, knows her bones, all the moments that led to this one. There really is no turning back, and the concerned Attendant who hovers nearby is a mere buzzing on the horizon. No one can help. She can collapse, die, or go on to whatever awaits.

Everyone stands before that uncompromising mirror. And after the anguish, anger, shock, and denial, we must wrap ourselves in the fabric of our fate and go on. Graham admired Picasso's work, and in *Girl before a Mirror* we see a similar moment. Picasso's girl looks fairly normal to the casual observer, but her inner self is purple and green, in chaos. Still, a rounded arm seeks to enfold all of her disparate parts and embrace them as the puzzle that she is. Those rounded, motherly arms of the Attendant try to nurture Herodiade time and again but are repulsed.

### Miki Orihara as Herodiade

"I am in some separate place inside of myself. It may be imaginary; I don't know. It may be a memory. The Attendant is there and I don't even know why she worries, why she wants to take my shoe.

"If I think of Martha and her fears of aging, I can see this for myself, too. As a dancer, I am getting older. Dance is an art that depends on the body. Other artists can keep their craft, their gifts forever. We all see our bodies changing. My changes in this dance itself reflect a time when I can turn emotion into motion. I really believe this. When you feel 'up,' your breath is up. So for me, even small movements in my body come close to Herodiade's struggle to release. I know the contraction is there. Without release, there is no contraction.

"Herodiade is contracting and releasing a period of her heart, her life. No one else can do this for her. My final moments onstage are ones of peace and acceptance, even adventure."

Miki Orihara as Herodias and Elizabeth Auclair as the Attendant in *Herodiade*

## Fang-Yi Sheu as Herodiade

Fang-Yi Sheu comes to the Herodiade role with great personal resonance. "This dance is my life. It is every artist's story. I struggle to find myself within my art, within my family, in Taiwan and here in New York. Here I am very alone, and I think my family would like to see me home in Taiwan. I must dance. I am very alive when I take Martha's dances into my heart. And so I must stay in New York and miss everyone I love in Taiwan. This is my sacrifice. When the woman looks into the mirror, I can hardly look with her. I am hoping to see my future, too. I talk to myself about this, and the ballet is my heart and soul on that stage."

Fang-Yi Sheu as Herodias in *Herodiade*

## The Attendant

The relationship between Herodiade and her Attendant reveals much about each woman. Two formidable Graham artists reflect on the Attendant.

Elizabeth Auclair: "As companion to Herodiade, I extend my arms, my heart to this woman. I am no mere servant. I love her. She knows this, but in this particular moment she cannot acknowledge this truth. If asked, I would do anything for her. In fact, she is far from me, and I can only do the simplest of tasks well for her as my homage of respectful love."

True in our life, this. Sometimes a glass of water, an open window, a cool cloth are all we can offer the suffering beloved. Please take this from me. I love you.

Katherine Crockett: "I think she wants to die. Surely not, I say. Let me help you. There must be other options. Will you let me hold you, put flowers in your hair? My fate is to witness this pain. I am not going away, and even if you push me off, I will be with you. I want to hold her like a mother would, but she is bent on mothering herself right now. She lets me put on her shoe as I have always done, and we both find a second of comfort in routine. The black cape she wraps herself in is her fate, and she stretches inside it and finally loses herself in it.

"I think of the pain of our lives and how the company of women can help us through. Caretakers dance a delicate dance from moment to moment. Where are we now? Any kind of transition is painful. This may in fact be about death, but I see birth, change, the next day of our lives.

"At one point she sits me down and says, 'This is it. Let me be. I am strong. I know this is the hard way, and I know I will suffer. Let's go.'

"Then, as the music shifts, I kneel and really hear her. She exposes herself in the white undergarment, and the ritual begins. There is something to do, a pattern, a protocol to follow. We storm angles and squares; we march with purpose. I plot out these concrete spaces. Then I lay out the cloth on the chair and take her dress, and for a moment I wonder if there is a last chance. But she has made her decision and executes a slow walk to the mirror. My character gives validity to Herodiade's voice by witnessing what really is a holy moment. Finally, she flies like wind through space. There is a window, and she flies through it to some place I cannot go."

The woman gazes into the unforgiving glass and moves through it to the new place that awaits.

She pushes the Attendant away. No time now for tears and embraces. That moment is past, and a solitary journey has begun. What will the pain be? Disease, death, age, a life for art above love, a voice no one else hears, hearts breaking, bodies failing us. Martha was dealing with all of these deeply personal issues herself, trying to reconcile the dancer's life with the craving for a maternal role as well. Within this dance she helps one discover how to mother and nurture oneself. The ballet touches on all the painful choices a woman must face.

Finally acquiescing, Herodiade allows the Attendant to prepare her for the ritual, for attention must be paid and steps followed in order. Stripping to an astonishing pure white garment, Herodiade looks upward, and her illuminated face is the last image we have.

She is gone.

## 14. *Deaths and Entrances*

Wind and rain sweep the English moors, and Emily, Anne, and Charlotte Brontë pace the rooms and drafty corridors of their remote parsonage home. Each sister experiences small deaths this evening and moves into her own memory cocoon many times. Time passes, but who knows how much? It may be seconds, minutes, or hours. We cannot tell. In *Deaths and Entrances*, three women remember past suitors who come to dance again. The women see each other through the prism of their shared childhood. Each in her own world relishes personally imposed privacy.

This magnificent ballet, restored in the 2005 season, offers dancers significant roles to explore over many seasons to come. Miki Orihara as Emily moves within the tortured sensibilities of the genius writer whose very intellectual gifts may suffocate her. Emily ponders possibilities, much like Hamlet, to the point where no choice seems viable. What decisions confront her? Shall she surrender to the comforting stability of her Poetic Beloved, one who will never desert her, or shall she listen to her passionate heart and give herself to the Dark Beloved, one who may be dangerous but who is fully alive? This split in the Romantic sensibility between passion and reason propels not only period literature but the very life of this dance's creator. Martha Graham agonized about how to balance senseless passion and sensible normalcy in her own life. Her choices were not always good ones.

As the Poetic Beloved, Tadej Brdnik moves with solicitous energy to assure Emily that he "will always be there." He explains, "I may be something like her brother, Branwell." His death decimated Emily Brontë and she died soon after his funeral. "She has no need to look for me; I am always waiting to catch her. She cannot hurt me or reject me enough to make me disappear. Now, I may not really be there at all, but she worries and worries about the degree of normal stability she needs in her life, whether it is romantic or day to day."

Persuasive argument, to be sure. Alas, an even more compelling counterargument exists. As the Dark Beloved, Christophe Jeannot is raw desire. "I want her to want me. I touch her, stroke her. I feel her, and I make sure she knows I will always come back." In every sense, this Dark Beloved is Heathcliff.

In *Wuthering Heights*, Catherine Earnshaw is the text for Brontë's schism. Drawn inexorably to the rough and passionate but penniless Heathcliff, Cathy knows that she is making the wrong choice when she agrees to marry the wealthy but mild-mannered Edgar Linton. With him, she will be the greatest lady in the land, but she will find no excitement or romance. Attempting to talk herself into her poor choice, she tries her argument out on the long-suffering housekeeper, Nelly Dean. Heathcliff, having just arrived, drenched by a storm on the black moors, overhears her say: "It would degrade me to marry Heathcliff now." He departs before he can hear her next, more heartfelt words: "Nelly, I *am* Heathcliff! He's always, always in my mind: not as a pleasure, any more than I am always a pleasure to myself, but as my own being."

Christophe Jeannot as the Dark Beloved in *Deaths and Entrances*

Miki translates this tearing apart in her dance. Her intense rendering of the role answers Martha's own question: "Haven't you ever been in a room where someone you loved, who no longer loved you, walked in, and your heart fell to the floor?" For Miki, the "Poetic Beloved is very comfortable. I never have to look for him. He is always there, ready, wanting to support and love me. In some ways, he is like a brother. The men move around me in the dance the way they do in my mind, each one crossing my line of vision, physically reminding me how hard this choice is. No one knows this but me. The issue is not solved."

A chess game with oversized pieces dominates stage left, and Miki notes, "I just can't make myself move a chess piece. That would be too final. I see the game; I just don't want to play. I am thinking many things at once. Objects in the room call me, and I look at them for some answers. Maybe my past will tell me what to do now. The seashell I hold takes me to childhood seashores. I also think I see the goblet of my destiny there, and one vial may hold the ashes of a dead ancestor. My body goes toward these things, and then some force jerks it back. I am prowling like a cat. This woman thinks too much. She is very intelligent, and she knows she can't have it all. It is pushing her to the edge. In conflict, I move from my center. Every movement relates to my back. I use the contractions as part of defeat and wait, wait for the release. I am creating my own space to exist in. As for the sisters, we rarely touch. They are probably jealous of me, and I do not think my answers are in either one of them. It is sad we can be in the same place but far apart, but it is true."

"I am still working out the relationship among the three sisters. Even though some of my movements suggest anger toward them, I am not angry. I want to prove myself to them, and I don't want to be told what to do. As I continue dancing this role, it will become clearer to me."

"My favorite part is the solo of my madness. I snap. I really like letting everything go. All the pressure has been too much, and I am trying not to lose control while I dance, but I feel myself slipping away. I don't care who sees me. The shudders come over me in waves I can't plan. Those terrifying falling spirals let me find even more private places. The choreography here is wonderful for a brave dancer. I try to come back to daily life and be 'myself' with the sisters, but too much has happened. I really want to be alone. I cannot let them see the real me, so I compose my face, my body."

The meandering maze of our minds takes us where it will. Martha scribbled a note in her journals about this, referring to Francis Bacon: "For he who recollects or remembers, thinks; he who reasons, thinks; and in a word the spirit of man, whether prompted by sense or left to itself, whether in the functions of the intellect, or of the will and affections, dances to the tune of the tho'ts."

Suitors drift into this maze, and as a cavalier Maurizio Nardi moves through the clouds of memory as perhaps "a dear memory for Emily. The clock of her memory is rotating, and she tries so hard to remember . . . who was that man? I can almost see him now." For Maurizio, it is clear that he is only in her mind, and his melting movements spill out into space, as the "One in Black" (Emily) pulls him in and out. "I work on upper torso and legs to create a nest where I can be pulled out by her magnetic thoughts."

Christophe Jeannot and Miki Orihara in *Deaths and Entrances*

Meanwhile, the other two sisters recall their own cavaliers. Does memory heighten or dull their suave appeal? Why did he dance with her and not with me? Did he really desire me, or was he just waiting for a chance at Emily? Sisters' jealousies linger and rankle, sometimes right up to the deathbed.

To find her character as Anne, the youngest sister, Virginie Mécène dipped into Martha's family and her own. Geordie, the youngest of the three Graham sisters, struggled for her entire life to keep up with her big sister. She never quite measured up, though, and clung to Martha until she died. Virginie incorporates this skittish quality in her many entrances and departures during this work. "There is an anxious sharpness to this sister, and I control her from the top of my spine. I am not comfortable around men; I am hiding, I am not confident. I have had to restrict my movement to create this character. The three dancers decided how to define each character. Often I move my head carefully to relate to the others, especially Miki as Emily. Strange postures occur, but they do seem to work with our Graham techniques." As Virginie dances, the eye wants to follow her. She captivates. She exceeds the dramatic requisites of this ballet.

The three Brontë sisters created the imaginary kingdoms of Gondal and Angria when they were children and wrote stories on bits of paper they hid in their pockets. Virginie also played at this with her three brothers and seven sisters in France. "We had 'Les Petits Papiers' in a cat-and-mouse game with scraps of paper. Remembering this game helped me to become a Brontë!" The youngest version of ourselves is always in the house to remind us who we were and how we grew. We are never truly adults when we go home. How did the child I was become the woman I am? All three sisters puzzle over this. In the puzzling night we witness, the women find themselves holding hands near the end. Startled, they pull away, and the chance to ask each other what memories overlap is gone. Aging sisters need to confirm their pasts in each other's eyes and stories. These sisters, for private reasons, deny themselves this comfort.

Virginie has mentally constructed an entire house, on- and offstage. "I imagine other parts of the house, and when I leave, I go someplace else. The house is large, and as the dance proceeds, I am in a room, somewhere, and sometimes I come into this particular room. A person looking in our window would see what could happen in any house. An hour, a day—we all live these moments."

After the final performance of *Deaths and Entrances* in the 2005 season, I walked home across midtown Manhattan with Miki Orihara. What was it like for her to create a role as though it had never been danced before, to make it hers? She smiled into the darkness. "Tonight, I went someplace new. I trusted myself to pull together all the advice, all the old films that are so fuzzy and blurred, all the past Graham dancers who told me how they saw this role. I left all that behind and let myself go. There was no choice. It just came to be."

These dances are not dead. They simply await souls to inhabit them in each dancing generation. Martha knew: "There are so many little deaths, those moments of doubt, loneliness, fear . . . moments when one ceases to be for a short time. Then there is the entrance again into the real world of energy that is the source of life, that is the immortality."

Virginie Victoire Mécène in *Deaths and Entrances*

# 15. "Spectre-1914," from *Sketches from Chronicle*

"Spectre-1914" constitutes one-third of the original *Sketches from Chronicle* created in 1936 and now lost. A ferocious response to fascism, this ballet was partially reconstructed into "Steps in the Street," "Spectre-1914," and "A Prelude to Action." In the course of the dance, a corps of women empower each other to confront the past horrors of war and death as they coalesce to change the future of the world. As they march and turn, sometimes together, sometimes alone, their power as part of the whole becomes evident, and a new future is visible before our eyes. It is exhilarating.

In "Spectre-1914," one woman sweeps a voluminous red and black gown up and down and over her head. Standing on a boxed platform, she lays forth the outrageous deeds of death and war from all time. Moving up and down, her height increases as the box itself supports her frame and the gown envelops all. She is impressive.

She is Fang-Yi Sheu. A diminutive woman with shy demeanor, she melts into the streets of New York. No one would guess the power surging within her. She can extend her leg upward impossibly. Bodies cannot do this; souls can.

She explains, "I just know what I have to do. Peace must begin with me. I feel the power of another world in this dance, in this dress. I can change the world.

"I do not know where this power comes from, but it is overwhelming and exhausting to let it run through my body. The skirt shows you the blood on your hands. Look! Savagery will destroy us! I extend my arms, my legs, but it is all of us onstage. I am just the one talking. You must listen to me! I am not afraid of anything. I can die. My energy pours out to you so you know you are not alone. I am with you.

"With all my breath, I speak to you. My whole past and future is here."

*If it be now, 'tis not to come;*
*If it be not to come, it will be now;*
*If it be not now,*
*Yet it will come—*
*The readiness is all.*
*—Shakespeare, Hamlet*

Elizabeth Auclair in "Spectre-1914," from *Sketches from Chronicle*

## 16. *Diversion of Angels*

With the lightest, tenderest of touches

Love comes to life.

Not lust, but a level of devotion, of deep touching

That says we are one.

It happens so fast.

And so, these six angels, with a light flutter of fingers dancing on air, bring couples to life.

Feet touch the ground

Tenderly

Separately

But complete—together.

I see you in a suspended gaze

And all is

Joy, light, air.

Surely this is what angels are like at play.

Serious, elegant play.

It starts with a flirtation, frisky young love, and its color should be yellow.

Perhaps this frolic turns deeper and more passionate. That couple, naturally, must be red.

Later, only the most fortunate move carefully into the circle that is simple, perfect, and white.

You surround me entirely and with these sweet rounds I seek

Time and space

For a new

Circle

Of me

Majestic yet light

Only ones who have lived as the young Couple in Yellow, the erotic Couple in Red, are ready to become the Couple in White. This is the place of deepest enduring love. Here, you are whole within yourself.

Martin Lofsnes and Katherine Crockett come together with the slightest of movements toward each other, like pieces of a puzzle. Martin wants his partner to "know that I will be with her forever, in every way. She is part of me."

Katherine strokes his chest and leans forward investing each movement with energy and space. "I am the goddess of that perfect stillness we share." Her solo highlighted by graceful tilted penchées links heaven and earth, and she seemingly derives power from the earth. Her archetypal presence evokes Egyptian paintings on the tombs of deceased loves. "I feel like Isis and Osiris. I am the one who knows the secret."

Martin Lofnes and Katherine Crockett in *Diversion of Angels*

# 17. *Satyric Festival Song*

From far upstage, a sprite in green and black stripes hops onstage sideways with her back to the audience. How did she get there? Martha Graham may have started this whimsical piece just this way, but we are not sure.

No films or notes survive to chronicle *Satyric Festival Song*. Martha always wanted to move on to the next dance without a backward glance. One day, of course, the dances stopped, and her company wanted to retrieve their dance legacy.

In 1994, former principal dancers Janet Eilber and Diane Gray collaborated to re-create this work. It was a puzzle hunt for clues.

"We had no music, just a scrap of the score for one instrument," recalls Janet. "We worked from the collection of Barbara Morgan photographs and tried to guess the sequence." Diane remembers "laying all the pictures on the floor and looking at the dancer's hair. If it swung to the left, we knew a movement had to come before and after." Tracing this vaporous dance was like viewing a landscape as a Japanese painter. One cannot paint the wind; one sees where it has been. Terese Capucilli helped by constructing a flip-book of photos like the ones seen in the early days of film. Movement by movement the dance began to emerge.

"I tried to retain the southwest flavor Martha admired and also to honor the gaudy, bawdy mood of the satyr dances of ancient Greece. It was meant to be fun, outrageous, and a little naughty,"

Janet continues. "When we had a rough structure assembled, we explored some new music and found we liked a composition by Fernando Palacios. It was light and sassy—just what we wanted."

All this may sound anomalous to audiences used to Martha as Grand Dame of Dance. Diane and Janet agree. "Martha was very funny. She had great timing and could work a room of people faultlessly. She had great wit—a wicked sense of humor. We tried to channel that laughter." Those laughs must have helped carry her through some trying years when her skills and health deteriorated. Her inner vision did not dim, though, and near the end of her life we see the whimsy of *The Owl and the Pussycat* and the raucous *Maple Leaf Rag*, where she actually parodies herself.

"We videoed the dance, using a tall girl from the school," Janet recalls. "I kept the floor patterns I saw, and then layered in comedic timing. I wanted friction, too, where the dancer rubs up against the music, masters it. The music can't be decoration. It all took about four to six weeks to finish. A character emerged with birdlike quickness. It was such fun."

Because of their creative reconstruction, Janet and Diane made a great contribution to dance history and preservation work. Now dance reconstruction toolkits are available to university dance departments eager to introduce a new generation of performers to the Graham oeuvre.

As her hair lashes back and forth, Miki Orihara personifies what Diane interprets as the artist as seeker. This is one "who completely dedicates body and heart to dance and finds joy in the decision." She springs back and forth; she turns her back on the audience and wiggles her bottom. In a flash, she peeks over her shoulder and asks if we saw that. Like it? And the dancer laughs with us, looks right into our eyes and laughs out loud. The fourth wall disintegrates, and we all are onstage together.

*Miki Orihara in Satyric Festival Song*

# 18. *Acts of Light*

With *Acts of Light*, Martha Graham culminated her rich life in dance. A few works would follow, but this ballet defines dance. No one has ever produced as many works for the stage as Graham. Unafraid to return to concepts and themes many times in her evolution, at the end of her career she crafted this parting gift for anyone who can see beyond movement into grace, anyone who can sway with joy. It is elegant, clearly articulated, and lovely, a paean to the human body in motion. It is her farewell.

Dancing to lyrical strings, the full company is onstage throughout the ballet. With initial moves in rondeau form of repeating circles, Martha absorbs classical ballet into her contemporary voice. There are only five positions in all the world of dance, and they are all here, blended with Graham floor work. These universal movements speak for a choreographer bold enough to blend past, present, and future. The first movement defines love. The central woman senses the male presence, pushes him away, then returns to him magnetically, erotically. He takes her in his arms and rocks her back and forth. She wants to surrender, and the climactic lift to his shoulders creates one new person. When they walk back to back, they are Adam and Eve; he carries her off in complete knowledge and trust. Eden has returned.

A sorrowful interlude gives pause. Loss and lamentation, central rivers to Graham's world, run through us again, but mitigated now. Unlike the gut-wrenching agony experienced in *Lamentation* or *Deep Song*, the pangs of this dance allow for release and flights of mercy. In a white, shroudlike garment, the central woman moves prayerfully and is finally carried off in a cross formation.

Miki Orihara in "Lament" from *Acts of Light*

Immediately, hope returns to the stage in the form of a beautiful sun god. Covered in shimmering gold, he stands center stage, arms and legs extended. He is Leonardo da Vinci's man in the center of the universe, and heavenly circles circumscribe him. Truly, he is the measure of all things.

So many beautiful bodies, refulgent in gleaming light! With runs, circles, cartwheels, in golden leotards that reflect sun and light, the company is reborn after the dark.

Each performance must finally end. In *Acts of Light*, after a final falling embrace, the lovers turn to the company. It is time. Now they turn to the audience, hands cupped outward. In their emptiness, they are full. We are receiving gifts from them. The dancers bow deeply, falling to their knees. When they bow, it is with humble gratitude. They thank us for sharing this fragile art that runs through their limbs. We last see them sitting in Buddha poses, arms extended, hands still open. All for us.

A ghost light remains onstage in every theater when the show is over and everyone goes home. A naked bulb burns in a tall lamp. Past performers watch over the house. Wherever this company dances, Martha Graham must joyfully move her spirit to whisper, "And . . . one . . . "

Her every dance is an act of light.

Alessandra Prosperi, Elizabeth Auclair, Christophe Jeannot, Maurizio Nardi, and Miki Orihara in "Helios" from *Acts of Light*

And the newest generation of dancers? What voices must they listen to? Once a young artist knows that dance is essential to life itself, that one has no other choice but to dance at any cost, support is waiting at the Martha Graham School of Contemporary Dance, the oldest continuous contemporary dance school in America.

In 1926 Martha Graham founded her dance company and school, living and working out of a tiny Carnegie Hall studio in midtown Manhattan. It was there that the dance principles she embodied became articulated in a fresh vocabulary meant to "increase the emotional activity of the dancer's body."

Now approximately 250 young dance artists study at the school in a variety of programs under the guidance of director Marnie Thomas. Some move directly to professional performance, while other paths lead to dance pedagogy. Aspirants study Technique, Repertory, Composition, Music, and a variety of elective classes. Working with Graham dancers from the 1940s to the current company, dancers have a unique opportunity to absorb many layers of Graham technique and philosophy. Pearl Lang, Linda Hodes, and Marnie Thomas worked with Martha during her prime creative years. They hold the text in their bodies. Past and present Graham dancers have a treasury to give willing students.

The dances are written in hearts, eyes, arms, and legs, but not on paper.

Current company members work generously with students and even, in Tadej Brdnik's case, mentor them into New York's rich artistic life. In the Young Artists Program, Tadej coordinates thirty high school scholarship students culled from throughout New York City and involves them not only in dance but opera, theater, and the city's museums in an effort to help them reach their artistic potential. A special link exists between Graham students and the Isamu Noguchi Museum.

Noguchi contributed sets and stage formations that drove right to the heart of Martha's themes. They stand onstage today as visual metaphors.

Tadej: "The arts all relate, and I want them to taste it all. This is my gift to all who helped me to realize my dreams. It started when a woman in Slovenia stopped me on a soccer field and told me I had rhythm and that I could dance. That moment changed my life."

Under the artistic direction of Company alumna Janet Eilber, Martha Graham Resources is collating all physical and intellectual resources required to sustain the Graham repertoire, creating new documentation to capture Martha Graham's legacy by making these assets available to students, professional dancers, researchers, journalists, and the public at large.

What will young students explore? Teaching voices speak to them:

"Your body is a vehicle enclosing emotion. Use it to make others feel."

"Movement never lies. It needs a core of truth."

With that philosophical base, technique follows. Form follows function.

Students explore their inner powers of expression, and their informed movements celebrate that awareness. Perhaps, if they listen carefully, they may sense Martha in the studio and hear her whispering:

"Move on a stationary base."

"Carve a place for yourself in space."

"Breathe. Contract. Release."

"Let gravity pull you to earth."

Miki Orihara with students at the Martha Graham School of Dance

Pearl Lang with students at the Martha Graham School of Dance

Tadej Brdnik with students at the Martha Graham School of Dance

"Project through space as if space were opaque."

"Contraction is ecstasy as well as despair."

"There must be complete articulation of the foot; all the bones of the foot must move."

"The hip bone must move as the jewel in the watch movement."

"Hold the movement, not daring to move, but moving."

"Lift your face as if you expect to be kissed."

After two years, the most promising candidates may find themselves in the Ensemble, the School's pre-professional student troupe that performs Graham works for schools and concerts. From there, a few move into the company itself, feeling privileged to be chosen. Jennifer Conley was one such dancer. Backstage before a performance, she reflected on her life in dance.

"I had an ordinary college experience until my sophomore year, when I called my parents and said I wanted to change my major from the College of Business to the College of Arts and Architecture to study modern dance. They were concerned, to say the least! That spring I saw an ad for the Martha Graham Summer Intensive Program, and my teacher really encouraged me to try it. By the second week of the program, a deep experience was beginning to unfold—it was as though every searching part of my personality had found a home. This was it. Now I feel rooted in this community. When we are dancing onstage in the larger group pieces, I feel us working together, like we are one body, one spirit."

Jennifer Conley and Blakeley White-McGuire joined the Company in 2002 as it came back to life. To young dancers across the world who may be drawn to the emotionally, intellectually, and artistically rich environment of the Martha Graham Dance Company, they say, "Follow your inner truth. Follow it wherever it leads you. Go. Listen to your heart. Don't let outside forces stop you. The struggle is absolutely worth it."

Heidi Stoeckley discussed a variety of her roles in earlier chapters. Here she opens her journal to us, sharing her private thoughts as a dancer who is maturing in the Company.

"I have pleaded with myself to believe in the extraordinary. I yearn to discover something new through Graham's work, which is to me the extraordinary. It is not that I think myself equal to her . . . for she was a true genius . . . nor that I believe I could ever create something of her magnitude . . . but I so strongly believe that I must build upon it . . . to ask whether and why it feels so true. We are all one soul growing closer to the truth, and we each must do our part to add to the whole.

"The ego likes to keep me from being honest, and it gives up a good fight, but the magic comes when I can let it go. When I can be fearless and know we are all human. I am raw onstage and find my comfort in it. I leave it all there and step away to continue in my life. It is a catharsis. It seems Martha will not refuse me, and in all my terror to stare at myself in the mirror of her roles, I find I cannot refuse her. She has made something that is far too real to the root of us to accomplish without going to our innermost beings. We can fail the work, but the work will never fail us."

# Resources and Suggested Reading

Campbell, Joseph. *The Hero with a Thousand Faces.* Bollingen series XVII. Princeton: Princeton University Press, 1973.

———. *Transformations of Myth through Time.* New York: Perennial Library, 1990

Dance Collection. New York Public Library for the Performing Arts, Lincoln Center.

"A Dancer's Journal: Learning to Perform the Dances of Martha Graham" <www.artsedge.Kennedy-center.org/marthagraham> (an interactive site created by Janet Eilber and the Martha Graham Resource Center).

de Mille, Agnes. *Martha: The Life and Works of Martha Graham.* New York: Random House, 1991.

Euripides. *Medea.* Trans. Rex Warner. In *Norton Anthology of World Masterpieces*, ed. Maynard Mack. New York: W. W. Norton, 1997.

Graham, Martha. *Blood Memory.* New York: Simon and Schuster, 1992.

———. *The Notebooks of Martha Graham.* New York: Harcourt Brace Jovanovich, 1973.

Hamilton, Edith. *Mythology.* Boston: Little, Brown, 1942.

Horosko, Marian. *Martha Graham: The Evolution of Her Dance Theory and Training, 1926–1991.* Chicago: A Capella Press, 1991.

McDonagh, Don. *Martha Graham.* New York: Praeger, 1973.

Sophocles. *Oedipus the King.* Trans. R. C. Jabb. In *Complete Greek Drama*, ed. Whitney J. Oates and Eugene O'Neill. New York: Random House, 1938.

Stodelle, Ernestine. *Deep Song: The Dance Story of Martha Graham.* New York: Schirmer Books, 1984.

Tracy, Robert. *Goddess: Martha Graham's Dancers Remember.* New York: Limelight, 1997.

John Deane's portrait, fashion, and dance pictures have appeared in numerous national and international magazines.

Since his collaboration with the Martha Graham Dance Company began with the Company's return to City Center in May 2002, the body of work they have produced together has been used in a wide range of media to promote the Company.

In the spring of 2004 he began working with the Boston Ballet, producing all the promotional images for their 2004–2005 and 2005–2006 seasons.

For a full view of John Deane's work, or to purchase fine art prints of many of the images found in this book, please visit his online portfolio at: <www.johndeane.com>

Nan Deane Cano, John Deane's sister, is an educator and author living in Los Angeles. She comes to the Martha Graham works with a lifetime of teaching in the classics and humanities. Her work has appeared in various periodicals, university publications, the *New York Times*, and the *Los Angeles Times*. This collaboration with her brother has been uniquely rewarding.